Love Is a Secret

The Mystic Quest

for Divine Love

by

Andrew Vidich, PhD

Energy Psychology Press
3340 Fulton Rd., #442, Fulton, CA 954439
www.EFTUniverse.com

Library of Congress Cataloging-in-Publication Data

Vidich, Andrew, 1953–
  Love is a secret : the mystic quest for divine love / Andrew Vidich. — 2nd ed.
  p. cm.
  Includes bibliographical references.
  ISBN: 978-1-60415-253-1
  1. Mysticism. 2. Love—religious aspects. I. Title.
  BL625.V46 2015
  291.4'22—dc20

Copyright © 2015, Andrew Vidich

The photographs on pages 18, 68, 110, 120, 150, 160, and 172 were supplied by Art Resource, New York, and Giraudon Paris. Photos from the Metropolitan Museum of Art, New York, on pages 58 and 178 are from the Fletcher Fund, 1963 and 1945, respectively; on pages 34 and 138 from a gift of Alexander Smith Cochran, 1913; on page 128 from the Rogers Fund and the Foundation Gift, 1955; on page 98 from a gift of Edward C. Moore, 1928; and on page 86 from a gift of Jeffrey Paley, 1975.

Cover design by Victoria Valentine
Editing by Stephanie Marohn
Typesetting by Karin A. Kinsey

Printed in USA
Second Edition

10 9 8 7 6 5 4 3 2 1

Dedicated to all illuminated beings
who have graced this earth,
and my own masters,
Sant Kirpal Singh Ji Maharaj,
Sant Darshan Singh Ji, and
Sant Rajinder Singh Ji Maharaj,
who poured out in limitless measure
the wine of God's love
on this unworthy soul

Contents

Acknowledgments vii

Preface ix

Introduction 19

CHAPTER 1
Universal Man: Stages in the Unfoldment of Love 35

CHAPTER 2
The Call: Love Emanates from the Heart of the Beloved 59

CHAPTER 3
The Valley of Intimacy: The Development of Remembrance.... 69

CHAPTER 4
The Valley of Sincerity: The Vale of Tears................................. 87

CHAPTER 5
The Valley of Separation: The Fire of Burning 99

CHAPTER 6
The Valley of Concealment: Expansion of the Heart.............. 111

CHAPTER 7
The Valley of Estrangement: The Three Faces
    of Renunciation 121

CHAPTER 8
The Valley of Unity: The One in the All and All in One 129

CHAPTER 9
The Valley of Ecstasy: Beyond Acceptance and Rejection 139

CHAPTER 10
The Valley of Bewilderment: Destruction of Ego 151

CHAPTER 11
Unending Oneness: The Ocean of Infinite Love...................... 161

CHAPTER 12
Death: The Final Beginning....................................... 173

Endnotes..179
References 185
About the Author...189

Acknowledgments

I would like to acknowledge the help and inspiration of a number of people in the preparation of this revised edition.

Thanks to Sandy English for typing the early drafts, to Art Stein for general comments, to my brother and mother for their review of the manuscript in the earlier stages, to Dawson Church for his general good council and excellent editing, to Stephanie Marohn for her superb copyediting, to Karin Kinsey for her typesetting, and to Victoria Valentine for the graphically stunning cover design of the book. Thanks, too, to Ruth Raziel, who commented on much of the material, to Barbara Carey and Tana Santa Cruz who typed later versions, and to Donna Ryan for her fine copyediting. I would finally like to thank Tamir, my wife, for her excellent criticism and editorial assistance.

All of these people and many others helped make this book a reality and without their help this book would never have seen the light of day.

I would also like to acknowledge my spiritual masters, Sant Kirpal Singh Ji Maharaj, Sant Darshan Singh Ji Maharaj, and Sant Rajinder Singh Ji Maharaj. Kirpal Singh (1894–1974) of

Delhi, India, began an intense search for a true spiritual master at an early age. For years he investigated the claims of yogis and saints representing many schools of thought. His search culminated in initiation by Baba Sawan Singh of Beas, India.

For twenty-four years, he studied under his master's guidance, and was chosen to succeed him in the spiritual line. Thereafter, he served as a spiritual master, initiating over 120,000 disciples throughout the world and authoring over twenty books. In 1974 he appointed Sant Darshan Singh (1921–1989) as his spiritual successor. Sant Darshan founded the Science of Spirituality organization, which now has over 1,650 centers worldwide. He was the author of several books of poetry, twice receiving the Urdu Academy award. In 1987, he appointed His Holiness Sant Rajinder Singh as his spiritual successor, and passed from this world in 1989.

Preface

It has been a joy to work on, and now to offer to you, a revised and updated edition of my research into the mystical experience of divine love, as described by the mystics from various religions and spiritual traditions. Although much in this book remains the same, I have changed significant portions and refined certain wording to reflect more accurately the intended meaning of the text. I have also sought to clarify and more fully describe certain states that, based upon critical feedback from friends and practitioners, needed greater elucidation.

As I mentioned in the original version, however, this book, though well documented, is not intended as an exercise in academic research. The journey we take is anything but theoretical. It embodies the fullest expression of human capacity and potential, and embraces experiences that can only be described as transpersonal or supraconscious. Wherever possible, these experiences are presented in the mystics' own words.

The preparatory work for writing this book involved several difficulties. I read innumerable texts to find passages that were suitable. Many mystical treatises were not available in English translation. Also, out of hundreds of texts available, only a handful deal directly with the actual experience of the mystic, around which this book revolves.

Most important, the experience of the mystic needs special attention and differs from a conventional, or ordinary, perspective. Unlike Western psychologies, which are more or less understandable to the average person, mystic psychology describes levels of transcendent experience that are virtually impossible to compare with commonly understood modes of behavior. It is often extremely difficult to clearly define and articulate in ordinary language the experience of the mystic. As language is but a feeble means of communication, I caution the reader not to mistake the moon for the finger that points to it.

This book is about the experience of divine love in the context of the lover-Beloved relationship. It does not attempt to be universal in application, because there are valid distinctions between spiritual disciplines. Nevertheless, I have made a conscious effort to show the uncanny similarity in experience between one religion and another. In addition, I have tried to indicate how, though the language may be radically different, certain other features reveal a hidden connection or deeper truth in common. This task was easier with religions that are predisposed to a devotional or, to use the Hindu term, *bhakti* approach.

Despite obvious differences between the outer forms of worship practiced, however, the central core of the mystic's experience in devotional faiths, such as Islam, Christianity, Baha'i, Hinduism, Sikhism, Jainism, and Judaism, is essentially the same. Buddhism and Taoism are considered exceptions by many theologians. Yet as different as their ideas may at first appear, their devotional essences are strikingly similar. Scholars who have pointed out lines of comparison include Angelus Silesius, the early sixteenth-century Christian mystic; Thomas Merton; and the twentieth-century Japanese mystic and scholar Toshihito Izutsu.

Since the publication of the first edition, however, a great deal of scholarship and research has provided more evidence along these lines. We now have the testimonies of mystical experiences of light well documented in near death experiences, pre-death visions, and radical epiphanies, as well as within the core writings of mystics and practitioners. The work of Wayne Teasdale and the Cypriot mystic Daskolos provides wonderful new vistas into the landscape of this all-encompassing experience.

The immediate purpose of this book was and still is to provide a working road map of the metaphysical psychology of this extraordinary relationship between the lover—the one approaching God—and God, the Divine Beloved, from its beginnings to its final consummation in union. A number of distinct states of consciousness seem common across all religious boundaries, whether devotional or not.

Some spiritual traditions might argue that all of these stages of attraction and love are illusory to begin with, for the entire outer world is illusory. From this perspective, the task of defining these transformations is merely labeling different aspects of illusion—clearly, a meaningless task. While I admit the ultimate ontological reality of this argument, such a statement can have meaning only if spoken by those who are themselves free from the bondage of illusion. It is very much like trying to lecture a starving man that his experience of hunger is an illusion and he should not waste his time searching for food, as the body is just another form of deception. In the end, our journey is not illusory but deeply meaningful and the basis of our conscious growth as humans.

The issue, and the focus of this book, is the real—indeed sometimes brutally real—experience of spiritual transformation. If this book does nothing else, it will surely eradicate the notion that the transformation of consciousness is child's play. As Kabir, the great fifteenth-century Sufi teacher said, "When the arrow of separation hits, there's no healing; sobbing and sobbing you live dying and rise groaning." The all too real transformation of the lover as a distinct separate entity into the image and identity of the beloved is a journey of immense, even cosmic proportions.

It remains somewhat of an enigma why since the release of the first edition of this book nothing similar has come into publication. On a personal level, time after time, I have been confronted by people who found in the text of the mystics included here a definitive corroboration and validation of their own inner journey. I am deeply grateful that this book has offered such struggling souls some light at the end of the tunnel.

It will be interesting for the reader to note that although the mystic's journey has as its goal eternal peace and bliss, much of the journey is filled with an experience that is a kind of blissful agony or excruciating joy. It is here that our English language falls short in describing these mystical experiences in ordinary terms. As these experiences are not part of the norm of human expression, I have tried to create a new language to help elucidate them. As the mystic advances, each new vista of spiritual insight reveals ever-deeper levels of mystical unity, which defy the experience of duality and the duality-laden language of separation and union. His Holiness Sant Rajinder Singh has beautifully summarized this experience: "The mystical journey takes us where opposites reveal themselves as one."

The suprapersonal nature of this experience often defies description or analysis, not only because of the failure of language, but also because the experience transcends our cognitive and rational faculties. For this reason, mystics often speak in terms of symbol and metaphor. But even metaphor carries a profound power when uttered by one who has actually experienced this transformation.

And this power is of immense value to others who are traveling the same path. The mystics may make us laugh, cry, dance, or sing, but whatever we feel, we are moved to a deeper level of understanding by their utterances. My own spiritual master Sant Kirpal Singh, a great twentieth-century mystic, used to say that "the saints' words were brief but always pregnant with meaning."

This book will be of inspiration and value only to those who have some interest in the spiritual path. It may have some value academically or theoretically, but that is a by-product and not the primary purpose. Rumi wrote, "My verses are like bread which is unleavened but by reading which the yeast of thought is applied; and by night they rise, and in the morning the bread of realization is found." In a similar way, this book provides the raw "bread upon which each of us must add the yeast of practice and contemplation."

Although this book looks at the experience of these stages of transformation in linear perspective, progressing in time from one state to another, not everyone experiences every aspect of the journey in the order given. In practice, progress may be fast or slow, direct or indirect, depending upon the perseverance, patience, steadfastness, and constitution of the lover. Nevertheless, amid all these varying conditions, an inner map emerges from which others may find guidance. And although ten stages through which the lover passes are identified, it is extremely difficult in the later stages to distinguish among them.

In many cases, as Meher Baba has noted, the "God-communed" or "God-absorbed" lover may have little or no awareness of his or her station. In fact, this is but natural as one loses one's egoic self and merges into the Divine unity. However, enough mystics and saints of all traditions have written of their experiences to give us a clear picture into the stages and states that characterize spiritual transformation.

I am indebted to a number of people for their valuable assistance in preparing this manuscript; however, the guidance and spiritual inspiration of Sant Darshan Singh deserves more than special mention. His guidance has been invaluable; without it this book would never have seen the light of day. Not only did he provide the initial structure and content, but he also continued to offer suggestions and review the book as it was in process. Sadly, he did not see the final copy before he left this world.

In late fall 1979, Sant Darshan Singh Ji appeared within while I was meditating and instructed me to come to India as soon as possible. I had no idea what was in store for me, but within a short period of time I was on my way. A day or two after I arrived in Delhi, Maharaj Ji called me to his residence and asked me to bring with me the compilation of teachings by the masters on various themes of love that I had been working on. These excerpts were taken from many sources. When I arrived in his small flat, I sat down alongside five or six others. Almost immediately, Master Darshan said: Please give me the book you have been working on." I handed him the loose collection of quotes. He glanced through the pages quite quickly and then abruptly returned them to me. For the next thirty or so minutes, he proceeded to critique my efforts.

Sant Darshan Singh discussed the fact that some of my excerpts were from highly restricted copyrighted sources and could have landed me in trouble. In my naiveté, I had completely neglected the political implications of some of the quotes I had excerpted. Throughout his detailed discussion and strident critique, he continued to look steadily and directly into my eyes. As he did so, a penetrating beam of radiant white crystal light entered my body and electrified me from head to foot. When he finally stopped, I could neither cry nor laugh, neither speak nor move. I sat frozen in a state of bewilderment. Words are inadequate to express the sublime nature of the state I experienced. I can only say that I was lifted into a state of inner freedom and emptiness. I experienced God working through the vehicle of Sant Darshan Singh in a most majestic and awe-inspiring form. A towering blaze of light embraced me. I felt filled with light.

Sant Darshan Singh then closed his eyes for ten to fifteen minutes. There was a total wondrous silence. When he opened them, he asked that someone start a tape recording, and he spoke in detail about the plan and purpose of a "new" book I was to write. What astonished me most was that after he was finished, he said: "Brother, these are not my words, but the exact instructions of Param Sant Kirpal Singh Ji that I have just received." Incidentally, Sant Kirpal Singh had left the earth plane more than three years before. Without further ado, Sant Darshan Singh stood up and graciously said good-bye to our group.

I left the room utterly humiliated, yet intoxicated with unimaginable bliss and joy. I felt as if my entire self had dissolved in the ocean of divine unity. I felt such exquisite bliss and yet I was not present in my old identity anymore. When I left his room, there was no longer any interest in writing any book! I wanted nothing to do with it; I felt pulverized. For the next four or five days, I could not talk, eat, sleep, or interact in a normal way. When I finally returned to being able to function as before, who "I" was had been significantly altered. I felt spiritually free and without desires. My innermost self had changed so completely that I no longer recognized who or what the former "I" had been.

When I returned to my room that evening, I realized it was no longer I who would complete this book, as I was clearly incapable, but the Master himself. As I have since seen, this has been entirely true at every step of this book's progress. He compiled and completed it long before I ever imagined it. As with most things in the field of spirituality, the greatest lesson seems to be humility first, humility second, and humility third.

Ten years later, the book entitled *Love Is a Secret* was finally published. With his immaculate grace, the book has served as a vehicle that has led many seekers to the path. This is entirely due to his grace, and if there is any truth to be found in the book, it is also a result of his unbounded mercy.

Any failures and lapses are entirely a product of my pen. I can only hope that readers will find the mystics' words as priceless a jewel as I have found them to be and, understanding their true import, translate them into an enduring reality in their own lives. We may have filled libraries with the words of these great teachers, but if we have failed to integrate them into our lives, we bring ourselves no closer to true love and joy than before.

As Sant Darshan Singh has so aptly said, "The acid test of all spirituality is the degree to which we live it." This, in a few words, is the message of the life of every great teacher—and of our own.

Following Page:

Christ on the Tree of Life
Academia, Florence, Italy

Originally executed for the Convent of Santa Clara in Florence in the early fourteenth century by Pacino da Bonaguido, this painting illustrates a religious text, the *Lignum Vitae,* by Saint Bonaventure. In the text, he traces the origin of the Passion and Glorification of Christ in twelve chapters. In this painting, they are represented as the twelve branches of a tree. At the top of the picture is Christ in Glory with the Madonna, and below them angels and saints. At the top of the Cross, between the prophets Daniel and Ezekiel, sits a pelican, traditional symbol of Christ's sacrifice. At the bottom of the picture are eight scenes from Genesis; above these on the left appear Moses and Saint Francis, and on the right Saint John and Saint Claire.

Introduction

Embrace every man as your very own,
And shower your love freely
Wherever you go.
—Darshan Singh[1]

Whether it is Shakespeare's Romeo and Juliet, the Psalms of David, or Wagner's Isolde, themes of love permeate our entire culture. The universal language of love transcends all the limitations of speech, culture, religion, and concept that separate human beings. It is hard to find a single life that is not touched in some way by love.

As we look at love, we see innumerable ways in which it finds expression. We are familiar with familial love, romantic love, platonic love, and brotherly or sisterly love. Human artistic expression bears testimony to the depth of our acquaintance with these various expressions of love.

There is, however, an expression of love that humanity as a whole has yet to understand and experience fully, and that is divine love, which is the love God has for us. Although many have had initial glimpses of this unique experience of love, humanity at large is still in its infancy in this respect. More often than not, we confuse the ecstatic experiences of divine love with outer forms of worship or, worse, with religious fanaticism. The unfortunate result of this confusion is religious intolerance and a loss of faith in the validity and existence of the mystical experience. Mystical love transcends all barriers of race, caste, creed, and even religion. It eclipses all other forms of love and, in fact, is the source from which all love arises. It is truly "unconditional" in the strictest sense of this word.

Despite the misunderstandings about its true nature, in recent years the experience of divine love has become familiar to a growing number of people. In a *New York Times* poll, over 30 percent of all Americans indicated that they have had a transcendent or religious experience of divine love. In past societies, this transcendent experience was often thought to be the exclusive province of a select priestly or religious class. And until recent times, our modern society has tended to treat mystical experiences with extreme skepticism and disapproval, as though they were a pathological deviation from normal human behavior. For their part, orthodox religions have treated reports of personal revelation with critical regard, and sometimes with outright hostility.

Yet in the face of rampant materialism, religious intolerance, and violence on a global scale, more and more people are awakening to the importance of spiritual love. Over forty years ago when I was initiated by my spiritual master His Holiness Sant Kirpal Singh, meditation was looked down upon and even scorned. Today we are in the midst of a global spiritual renaissance and reawakening. Hundreds of millions of people, regardless of religious background, are seeking a direct experience of this divine love through meditation and contemplation. And there is a growing body of written works on meditation, yoga, and near death experiences.

Human and Divine Love

Through personal experiences of illumination, we can glimpse the experience of divine love. From the perspective of the mystic, all forms of love, whether divine or mundane, have as their source the unconditional love of our Creator for His creation. This divine love emanating from our Source expresses itself as the spontaneous attraction between two objects or beings, and finds its ultimate resolution in union.[2]

A great saint once remarked, "Love must love and a lover must have a beloved." Without an object of attraction, love remains dormant and latent. Whether that object is an attractive man or woman, a friend, or God, love must have a point of magnetism. We might assume that the mystic considers divine love the only valid form of love. Nothing could be further from the truth. The true sage emphatically states that all love, at whatever level, is a reflection of God's very essence or being.

In the East as well as in the West, a "spiritual love" is understood to exist when both lover and beloved transcend the limitations of merely physical or personal satisfaction in order to reach a state of spiritual oneness. Such love is purified of all self and selfish limitations. When it reaches its height and perfection, the lover is completely subsumed in the Beloved. He indeed has become the Beloved, for in perfect divine love all barriers and differences are completely swept away.

From a mystical point of view, the soul, which is a part of God, must eventually return to its source, for its essence is love as well. In the Qur'an, it is written: "To Allah we belong and to Him we shall return" (Surah Al Baqarah 2:156), meaning that all creation must eventually return to its Creator, for it is from Him that we have been created. This material realm is foreign to our essence and no one can stay here for very long. One day, we all will receive the "eviction notice."

From this perspective, our entire spiritual journey is to learn the inescapable truth that we are love itself and must return to the Source of all love. But to do so, we must be recast in the image of love; indeed, we must become Love itself. This idea of love is the universal paradigm upon which all experiences of love, whether human or divine, ultimately depend.

The Original Love Myth

In the West, the original myth to explore romantic love in all its pathos was the epic tale of Tristan and Isolde. It was the first story in Western literature that dealt with romantic love. Robert Johnson, author of *We: Understanding the Psychology of Romantic Love,* suggests it is the source "of all our romantic literature from Romeo and Juliet down to the love story in the movie in the local cinema."[3]

Like all great myths, the story of Tristan and Isolde has the power to uplift us. It pulls us out of our petty and limited lives and into a grander and fuller vision of reality. Unlike many other great myths of both the East and the West, the myth of Tristan and Isolde is a profound expression of our Western psyche. This makes it a good introduction to the psychology of the mystic and his or her relationship to the Divine Beloved.

The troubadours were poets and musicians, often of knightly rank, who were most active between the eleventh and thirteenth centuries in France and Italy. If we look at their enduring tradition, we see expressed, perhaps for the first time, a way of love that seeks not only a physical union with the Beloved, but also a spiritual one. The lover is willing to forsake the physical relationship for a greater spiritual love.

In Tristan's day, it was commonly believed that the world of the soul was to be gained, literally and symbolically, by sacrificing the desires of flesh. Terrible sufferings, anguish, and pain were all viewed as part of the transformative journey. What was this journey? It was the journey of the soul through the vale of tears. The unmitigated despair and suffering of the protagonists in romantic tales of that era were made bearable by the beauty, happiness, and perfection of the world into which they expected to enter.

Suffering, Death, and Transfiguration

The Cathars, an ascetic Christian sect contemporary with the troubadours, shared their belief that the path to the Divine Beloved necessitated suffering. They and the troubadours flatly stated that they were seeking entrance to the inner worlds through their passionate love. In most instances, they hoped to achieve spiritual beatitude by their physical death, because it released them from the slavery of the flesh. Passion, whether for a human or a Divine Beloved, gave them a foretaste of the ecstasy and yearning of the world to come. Romantic love was for them an initiation, a steppingstone to a higher, more glorious vision. In this respect, their view of courtly human love paralleled the medieval view of spirituality. The inner worlds could be attained only through suffering, the ecstasy of their passion, or death.

If we look into the true meaning of the word "romantic," we find that, epistemologically, it means one who has empathy or respect for the inwardness of others. It was precisely this inwardness with which the romantic lover strove to identify; when he was successful, he did indeed achieve a state of transcendence of himself and his limited world. The woman he loved was idealized into the symbol of all beauty and perfection and, indeed, in later centuries, was worshiped as Eros herself. Through Eros, goddess of love and symbol of perfect beauty, the lover was transfigured and transformed into the image of the beloved.

The whole tradition of romantic love, though greatly different today, has its grounding in the love and suffering of Tristan and Isolde. Today we fail to see our search for human love in this noble context, and yet all of us long for the perfect relationship that will fulfill us completely. Robert Johnson suggests that we are all on this quest, whether we see it consciously or it remains an unconscious archetype directing our lives.

Every culture has created its own mythologies around love. The quest for the Divine or Supreme Beloved is the great symbol, the great metaphor for the awakening of the soul. It is hard to find anyone who is not in some way or another seeking relationship. It is hardwired into our genes. From the moment we open our eyes in this world, our life is defined by relationship. Even the most hardened criminal has in his soul this innate longing for intimacy. The difference between the mystic and the early troubadours is that the mystic chooses a beloved who is the very personification of God, the incarnation of formless perfection. Saint John tells us: "The Word was made flesh and dwelt among us" (John 1:1–5).

The early troubadours did the same thing by personalizing, in the form of their cherished lover, the ultimate, perfect ideal of the beloved. This symbol of the perfection of their love ignored the temporal and spiritual shortcomings of the actual person. Yet the personal sufferings of the mystic and the troubadour are strikingly similar. They represent the pain of every mortal who tries to give birth to the highest potentials within oneself.

De Rougemont speaks of the psychology of romantic love when he asks us:

> Why is it that we delight most of all in some tale of impossible love? Because we long for the branding; because we long to grow aware of what is on fire inside of us. Suffering and understanding are deeply connected; death and self-awareness are in league; and the European romantics may be compared to a man to whom sufferings, and especially the suffering of love, are a privileged mode of understanding.[4]

For us in the modem world, the path to higher consciousness is no different than it was for the mystic of two thousand years ago or the troubadours of eight hundred years ago. The price for perfection is always the same, and that is the purification of all selfish and self-limiting behaviors. For pure gold to be extracted, it must be heated to a very high temperature, and then the foreign substances fall away. In a similar way, through suffering, trial and tribulation, we are purified of all dross and materialism. We may not want to admit that love is often painful and difficult, but in our heart of hearts we know it to be so. The irony is that we are, in fact, not giving up anything that is real, for the only real thing in this universe is love, for it alone survives.

The difference for us today is that most of us have failed to initiate consciously this quest for our highest potential. Rather, it is initiated for us by our latent unconscious needs for completion and lasting happiness. We project all our ideals of love, perfection, and beauty onto our husband or wife or lover who in the end can never fulfill those demands. The mystic tells us we could instead turn within ourselves to the Divine Beloved who alone can bring us to perfect completion and fulfillment.

In the West, we are used to "falling in love." This initial attraction is so strong precisely because it reminds us of an ideal of perfection. In time, realizing the impossibility of this ideal in the shortcomings of our partner, we become bitterly disappointed. As Robert Johnson so artfully puts it, we "follow our projections about always searching for the one who will match the impossible ideal and will magically give us transformation."[5] When we don't find the divine world in our loved one, we suffer and fall into despair.

When Antoine de Saint-Exupéry said, "Love is not so much looking into each other's eyes as it is looking in the same direction," he summarized the whole paradigm of the mystic. For the mystic, love is not something one falls into or out of. By its very nature, such a thing would be impossible. For the mystic, love is about "self-sacrifice and service." The mystic and poet Sant Darshan Singh summarized the goal of all true lovers when he proclaimed:

Very different from us, my friends, are those
who grieve for themselves;

Ours is the heart which hears the sorrows
of the world.[6]

The goal of the true lover is to completely and continually sacrifice oneself for others. Why? Because a true lover sees the image of the Beloved in every atom of creation. The fifteenth-century teacher and poet Kabir said it in similar words: "Love is giving, giving, and still more giving."

When Dr. Mohammed Iqbal, poet laureate of India, was asked by his friend Sant Darshan Singh the meaning of the word "love" in his verses, he replied, "When I speak of 'love' I mean 'a continuous struggle, a continuous restlessness.'"[7] For the lover of the Divine Beloved, love is a continuous restlessness of the heart. It is a constant yearning for greater perfection and greater selflessness.

The Bridge between Inner and Outer

The true lover is unaware, ironically, of the love that flows through him or her. Such a lover's life is shaped by the needs and hopes of others. For such a one, all creation is revealed to be the very image of the Beloved and, therefore, the closer one approaches the Beloved, the more ardent the desire to give of oneself selflessly. What this implies is that, for the divine lover, every act must reflect the love in which one lives and moves.

For the lover who has bestowed his or her affection upon a competent spiritual teacher or guide, the very first place in which the process of transformation must occur is in the home, among those closest to one. The spark of love given by such a teacher manifests first in love of parents, spouse, and community and is, in fact, what makes divine love a possibility.

One Sufi poet said, "The phenomenal is the bridge to the real." Without the experience of the phenomenal world, the numinous world can never be approached. The mystics' message throughout the ages has been a call to awaken to the deepest levels of love within us. When love is awakened in our inner being, our perception of the universe undergoes a vast change. From this new vantage point, the mystic sees everything endowed with love. Even the stars, sun, and moon are seen to move and orbit out of love. Mystics have stated that love is not only the driving energy behind all creation, but also the purpose of its existence. It is the force within humankind that has sought unity with God since the dawn of creation.

Mystics maintain that, as we are creations of God, and God's essence is love, it is in our very nature to love. Sant Kirpal Singh remarked, "Love is innate in our souls; we need only awaken it." Thus, if there is a difference between divine love and the love of human beings for each other, it is not in nature but in degree. Human love always contains an element of selfishness. Divine love, in its purest form, is totally selfless. Divine love embodies a state of self-transcendence in which every trace of the lower self is completely removed. What remains is the universal expansive and eternal Self, which is a part of God.

Consider the example of a father who loves his son. He cares for his son, gives him the best education, clothing, and financial support, but does so with the idea that his son will one day become successful and help him in his old age. If the son does not succeed, the father becomes disappointed and loses interest in his son. Tainted by selfish motives, his love falls short of being selfless. This love has noble aspects to it but is not free of the lower self. This love might better be termed love mixed with ego or desire.

Yet another kind of love is the love between a mother and her child. In this case, we have a mother who devotes her entire life to her child, giving up everything for her child's best interest. Even if the child does not live up to her expectations, she still goes on loving the child, caring for the child's welfare, and giving more and more of herself. However, if the mother were to see a similar child on the street, one who is uncared for, unwanted, and destitute, she might not respond with the same love she gives her own child. This shows that her love is limited to her child, the source of her personal interest and pleasure. Her love is a love colored by an aspect of selfish motivation.

Divine love, however, lies far beyond the scope of the personal self, for it seeks nothing for itself. It is a love that is totally self-giving and not self-seeking. Sant Darshan Singh has suggested, "Love has only a beginning; it has no end."[8] Viewed from this angle, divine love is characterized by a total absence of self; it is a love in which the lover is totally replaced by the Beloved. It is a love that has no existence outside of the Beloved and no individual will of its own. It is a love devoid of ego, embracing the entire cosmos from atom to starry welkin. It has no limits because love itself, like God, is limitless.

The Ten Stages of Love

This book is organized around ten unique stages of divine love, distinct psychological states that characterize the mystic's journey. These stages first came into existence at the dawn of time but have rarely been articulated in modern times.

Chapter 1 introduces the concept of God as the ultimate source of love, whether human or divine, and the human soul as an essential part of God's essence. As the Bible states, "So God created man in His own image, in His image he created him" (Gen. 1:27), and that image was of course not physical but spiritual or the reflection of His own attributes. God, in His absolute state, exists as pure love; but in order to experience Himself, He projects Himself out as creation or, as the Holy Qur'an, has said, "From one He wished to become many" (Surah 2:117).

Inherent in this outward projection was the simultaneous attraction of the soul to returning to its original source. To facilitate this process of return, God manifests in the form of a God-personified being who is the very reflection and perfection of all God's attributes and qualities.[9] Such beings have been called by various names in different scriptures. Among the better-known ones are Christ, Messiah, Buddha, Satguru, Murshid-i-Kamil, and Master. It is this God-man, or Rasul (which literally means "mediator"), as the Sufis have called Him, who mediates and arranges for the return of the soul to its condition before the "envelopment in mind and matter."

The perfect love of the God-man, who is himself a perfect reflection of God's love, awakens in the would-be lover a longing to return to his or her original condition of perfect love and divine unity. The spiritual master first attracts the heart of the lover by showering him or her with ecstasy-producing glances. These glances, being filled with the love of God, inebriate the lover and draw him or her gradually "into the lap" of the God-man. Once enamored of the master, he or she becomes absorbed in the loving remembrance of the Divine Beloved. This stage has sometimes been referred to in mystic terminology as becoming "lost in the tresses of the beloved." William Butler Yeats, in his poem *Sailing to Byzantium* describes this unique attraction of the soul to the inner master:

> *O Sages standing in God's holy fire*
> *As in the gold mosaic of a wall,*
> *Come from the Holy fire, perne in a gyre,*
> *And be the singing-masters of my soul.*
> *Consume my heart away; sick with desire*
> *And fastened to a dying animal*
> *It knows not what it is; and gather me*
> *into the artifice of eternity.*[10]

As the lover's yearning for the beloved increases, the experience of separation becomes so painful that death itself appears desirable. Abdullah Muhammed depicts the agonizing plight of a woman caught in the pangs of separation from God: "The yearning for the Divine Beloved is consuming me. I am tired of this life and wish to purchase death in the marketplace." Ironically, death for the lover is not an undesirable fate. Rather it is the consummation of the endless restlessness and bottomless desire for the vision of the Beloved.

Succeeding chapters explore the relationship between divine love and lust, and the gradual abandonment of the latter in favor of the former. "Lust" is here taken to mean not only physical desire, but also all the entangling pleasures of the senses. Such desires turn the face of the lover toward the world and therefore away from the face of God. When human consciousness is attached to material enjoyments, it is wrapped up in lust or egotistic desire. Conversely, when individual consciousness attaches itself to its Source, which is God, divine love will result. Love may begin in the flesh, but it ends in the spirit. Lust, on the other hand, begins in the flesh but also dies there.

The Culminating Stages: Divine Madness and Ecstasy

In the last few of these ten stages, we see the lover gradually becoming completely lost in a state of divine ecstasy. At this point, the lover, having tasted the ineffable oneness of divine love, is unable to leave it. Every minute one longs to be in the presence of the Beloved who is the source of limitless joy and illumination.

Ibn al-Farid, a Sufi poet and mystic of the thirteenth century, aptly describes this wine, which intoxicates the lover: "If they watered the earth of a tomb with such a Wine, the dead one would recover his soul and his body revive."[11] The effect of this "wine" cannot be fully described in words, for it is an experience with no earthly equivalent. Not only is this divine wine a source of permanent peace and inebriation for the lover, but it also lifts the lover out of the prison house of rational and logical modes of understanding.

Plato tries to capture the difference between these states when he says, "The madness that comes of God is superior to the sanity which is of human origin."[12] This state of "divine madness" or transcendent wisdom results from an inner intoxication by "spiritual wine" and is not illogical but supralogical. Looked at through the mystic's eyes, the "wisdom of the world is foolishness before God" (I Cor. 3:39 NASB).[13]

This seeming madness, or more truly "mindlessness," shatters the veils of phenomenal existence and must perforce appear to the world as insanity. Jalaluddin Rumi expresses the lover's predicament eloquently: "It behooves us to become ignorant of this worldly wisdom: rather we must clutch madness."[14]

This "mindlessness" is the root of the tree of wisdom and prophecy. John Smith, the Platonist, acknowledged this state when he said, "There must be some kind of [madness] in all this prophecy."[15] But this mindlessness is, in fact, a sort of mindfulness of insight, for it is only through transcending the rational mind that real wisdom and prophecy can unfold.

In the final stages of extreme separation, we see the lover seasoned to live in a state of restless longing, pain, and anguish. Paradoxically, when this "torment" starts becoming a cure for the lover's pain, he or she begins the slow process of merging into the Beloved and ultimately becomes one with Him. Ghalib, the famous Indian Urdu poet, has tried to render this inexplicable state in words:

When your sorrows exceed all limits,
You become accustomed to those sorrows,
And once you become accustomed to those sorrows,
They become a part of your life.

Hazrat Baha, a Punjabi mystic, has said, "Let every hair of mine be an eye, and let every hair have a million eyes, so that I can look at the grace and beauty of my Master." Sant Darshan Singh has explained that we must become all eyes like the narcissus and, once having become all eyes, we will see the beloved in every eye.[16]

Gradually, a turning point comes when the lover loses all limited self-identity and merges completely into the Beloved. One no longer "sees" the Beloved; one begins to become the Beloved. When this stage is reached, one may look into the mirror, but find only the image of the Beloved there, not one's own image. Mystic literature is replete with stories and anecdotes of this often-misunderstood state. Allegory or metaphor is used to describe a condition that cannot be adequately conveyed by ordinary language.

The greatest romance in classic Persian literature is that of Leila and Majnun. In this epic, we find an excellent example of the use of metaphor for the spiritual journey. As it is told, after long and torturous periods of separation in which Majnun has literally wasted away in the desert awaiting his beloved Leila, she returns. To her dismay, she can no longer recognize him. His sufferings have reduced him to less than a skeleton, more ghost than human.

As she listens closely, she hears an unfamiliar voice repeating her name, coming from a tree. She looks more closely, and a strange, emaciated figure emerges from the base of the trunk. She cries out, "I am myself, Leila, and who are you?" Hearing these words, Majnun goes into a state of shock and says, "If you are Leila, then who am I?" His longing has led him to identify totally with his Beloved. After uttering these words, he gives an anguished shriek and dies.

The Final Stage: Unending Oneness

When love reaches such climaxes, the lover dies to his or her own limited identity. Love then is beyond the reckoning of the rational mind; only experience will capture it. At this point the lover no longer exists. Or if one exists, one exists in name only. Now the Beloved Himself has taken up residence in one's heart. At this divine banquet, where lover and Beloved unite, mystery after mystery is laid open, and the dualism of object and subject, of knower and known, ceases. Only the full beatitude of love remains. This experience is neither exterior nor interior, but wholly present simultaneously. Saint Bonaventure (*Itin Mentis*, 5) explains this paradox of unity consciousness by saying: "God's center is everywhere. His circumference nowhere."[17]

From this "center of eternity," which is the inner core of our being, all of us are being called by love. And it is this call that is heard again and again in the heart of the lover. Attar, a Sufi poet and mystic of India, echoes this call, which is the basis for our very existence:

> *In love no longer "Thou" and "I" exist.*
> *For self has passed away in the beloved.*
> *Now will I draw aside the veil from Love,*
> *And in the temple of mine inmost soul*
> *Behold the Friend, Incomparable Love.*
> *He who would know the secret of both the worlds,*
> *Will find the secret of them both is love.*[18]

Following Page:

Leila and Majnun in the Desert
Metropolitan Museum of Art, New York

In this beautiful depiction of the love story of Leila and Majnun from the *Khamseh of Nizami* (Mirror of the Invisible World), Majnun meets Leila in the desert after a period of the most intense agony and separation. Here Majnun is reduced to a ghost of a skeleton while singing his heartrending songs to Leila. The two lovers gaze upon each other with joy and wonder, as they had when they were children. For the mystic, this story illustrates the fire of separation, which consumes everything, including the lover's body and soul in desperate longing, as well as the supernal joys of union.

Chapter One
Universal Man:
Stages in the Unfoldment of Love

Whenever I travelled from earth to milky way,
I met love at every step and beauty in every glance.
—Darshan Singh[1]

In almost every scripture, whether of the East or the West, the human being is represented as the microcosmic symbol of the metacosmic being. All states of consciousness, from the atom to the absolute, are contained in and latent in the form of a human. The human soul comprises within itself all possibilities as well as all forms of manifest existence, from the humblest rock to the highest deity. The human being, according to Sufi belief, is the symbol of universal existence, the most perfect manifestation of God on earth, the prototype of God in human form.

Different traditions have variously described this prototype as the *Al-insanu-al-Kamil* or Perfect Man (Sufism); Archetypal Man or *Adam Qadmon* (Kabbalah); *Satguru,* Master of Truth (Hinduism and Sikhism); "Word made flesh," Christ and Logos (Christianity); and *Chun Jen* or *Wang* (Taoism). All exemplify the being that has fully realized the richness of all of life and the sum total of all possibilities latent in unmanifest Being. The perfect expression of these potentialities is a gift of pure love, translated by God's love into the created world of forms.[2]

This manifestation of perfect Love in the being of the Perfect Man is the first gift of love of the Absolute. The primordial Adam is none other than the first spark of love to descend into the world of time, the "I Am That I Am" from which all souls originate. Meister Eckhart, the thirteenth-century Christian mystic, affirms this truth when he writes:

When the soul strips off her created nature
there flashed out its uncreated prototype.[3]

Paradoxically, then, the soul's return to God is a return to itself, for all souls actually preexisted in God. According to Islamic tradition, at the moment souls were created, God asked them a question, "Am I not your Lord?" The souls replied in the affirmative, "Yes, You are our Lord." This moment, known as the moment of *Alast,* is the beginning of beginnings for created souls.

Al-Hallaj was a tenth-century saint put to death for his beliefs. He is sometimes known as the martyr of love. During a moment of spiritual elevation, he expressed this truth:

I saw my Lord with the eye of the heart. And I said, "Who are you?"
He answered, "You."[4]

"To see the world in a grain of sand and eternity in a flower" is not just the work of the poet; it is the vision of the mystic. For the mystic, the inward becomes the outward, for the mystic sees the divine unity revealed in everything. More correctly stated, the microcosm "is" the macrocosm. His Holiness Sant Rajinder Singh makes a similar point when he says, "The mystical journey takes us where opposites reveal themselves as one."[5] The outer world is a reflection of the inner world, which is the lasting reality beyond decay. What we perceive is a kind of magic show that, while seemingly real, is disappearing even as we experience it. The *Zohar,* the book of Jewish mystical teaching, says: "God made this terrestrial world in the image of the world above; thus all which is found above has its analogy below...and everything constitutes a unity."[6]

Mystics from all cultures and times have alluded to the divine imprint in manifestation and pointed out that every creation, however small, corresponds to a higher celestial ideal. For the mystic, all things are teachers. There are, as Shakespeare said, "tongues in trees, books in the running brooks, sermons in stones, and good in everything" for those who see the divine correspondences. In the Kaula Tantra, it is said, "From Brahman to a blade of grass all things are my gurus."

We human beings stand in a unique place in our similitude to the Creator. We are like a glass that is both translucent and transparent, radiating and reflecting simultaneously the perfect light and love of the Creator. In the Bible, this correspondence is alluded to in a number of places but most clearly in Genesis 1:27: "So God created man in his own image, in the image of God he created him; male and female he created them" (ESV).

Love: The Perfect Path

God is Love, the soul is love and the way back to God is also through Love.

—Param Sant Kirpal Singh Ji Maharaj

The human being is, in brief, the microcosm of the entire universe who participates in the infinite qualities and being of God to the extent that he or she realizes that potential. This innate affinity with God is expressed and embodied most clearly in the essence and manifestation of love. The divine correspondences are most perfectly realized in and through the medium of love, because our essence is love. The call to love is a call already latent within us as divine love.

Sant Kirpal Singh confirms this truth when he states that, as our own essence is identical to God's, and as God's essence is love, the most perfect method of return to God is through love. The path, then, can only be one of love, for: "There is no goal beyond love, because love is both the beginning and the end of the path. In this way, love and our own Soul are identical, for one who has divine love has reached God."[7]

The poet and saint Misbah-ul-Hayat spoke of this identity of the Divine Beloved with the lover as well:

The Almighty loved Himself if ye should know,
Made the universe His own mirror to see Himself aright
Displayed His beauty to Himself,
Really He is the lover, Beloved and love itself.[8]

The movement of the separate ray of the soul back to its primal and original source is a journey through the veils of ego and limitation to selflessness and infinite power. An individual's spiritual unfoldment is marked by a number of stages and states associated with acquiring the unique attribute of spiritualized love. There are many ways in which love can be made manifest in the outer world. In a similar way, spiritual love takes many different forms and expressions as it moves ever closer to its source.

In the Hindu Bhakti tradition there are essentially four degrees of spiritual relatedness that the disciple must traverse in order to attain the highest perfection of spiritual union. The Bhakti sage Shrivatsa explains that a disciple first has the relationship to Krishna as master (*dasya*). This gives way to filial respect (*vatsalya*), then to deep, intimate friendship (*sakhya*), and finally to the lover-Beloved relationship (*madhurya*), which culminates in the total realization of the Beloved.

The Christian and Islamic/Sufi traditions have also categorized this love into a variety of inner stages, each with its own unique requirements and expressions. This progression, catalyzed by worldly circumstances and inner aspiration, involves a gradual increase in devotion, faith, sacrifice, and unity with the Beloved. It is in this final relationship, however, in which the soul relates to God as a Beloved, that the inward journey of final realization is consummated.[9]

The Sacred Marriage

All souls are in fact female in relationship to God, for it is in our capacity to receive—to be emptied of everything—that we move into the divine embrace with the Divine Beloved.

In the Christian tradition, we have innumerable examples corroborating this point. The church, or communion of the faithful, is referred to in the New Testament as the "bride of Christ." Cardinal Newman also used the analogy of a wedding to describe the individual's connection with God when he said, "If a man wants the full bliss of contact with God, let him behave as a wife."

Saint John of the Cross prayed in similar fashion:

O my God, make me Thy wedded wife;
Unless You take me in Your embrace,
I can have no peace, no bliss.

When Saint Francis of Assisi saw the astral or light form of Christ, he called out, "Oh my dear husband, You have wedded me." Finally, we have the unambiguous words of Saint Catherine: "I am already wedded to a most noble spouse and shall never bestow my love on a human being."[10]

In the Sufi tradition, love in its mature state is always depicted as longing for the Divine Beloved. Jami, a thirteenth-century Sufi master and poet, cries out for the Divine Beloved in tones that make our mortal cares seem insipid:

Better to catch one moment's glimpse of thee,
Than earthly beauties' love through life retain.[11]

Or again, in the poetic revelry of Sheikh Ahmad al-Alawi:

Closer drew herself toward me,
raised the cloak that hid her from me.
Made me marvel to distraction,
bewildered me with all her beauty.
She took me and amazed me,

and hid me in her inmost self,
Until I thought that she was I,
and my life she took as ransom.[12]

Love in the temporal world, through whatever phenomena it is expressed, forms the foundation and support for the divine marriage that is consummated in the heart. This love is the perfect prototype for the lover's union with the Divine Beloved. Meister Eckhart draws us to this realization when he says, "As there is wedlock between a man and wife so there is wedlock between God and the soul."[13] Rumi, speaking of his ecstatic union with his beloved teacher Shams i-Tabriz, to whom he addressed thousands of his poems, sums up the union of lover and Beloved when he says, "I do not wear a shirt when I sleep with the Adored One."

This sacred marriage, consummated in the bed of the innermost heart, implies the deepest of mysteries. This divine marriage is a spiritual resurrection, but it also implies an end to our limited illusory ego. The word "marry" (*eko bhu,* in Hindi) means "to become one," but it also means "to die." This divine marriage implies the death of our separate existence, because until we have become consumed by the divine splendor, we cannot be fully united with the Beloved.

Such a marriage implies resurrection as well, because in this death there is full identification with the eternal Beloved. We are immortalized in the eternal spirit, which can never die. In the path of love, the lover soon realizes that there is no room for duality. Consummation of the spiritual journey is attained when lover, Beloved, and love are transformed into one essence. Abu Said ibn Abi 'L Khayr says:

Lover, Beloved and Love am I in one,
Beauty and Mirror and the Eyes that see.[14]

The path of spiritual realization, viewed from the lover's perspective, is a divine alchemical process of transmuting the mind-ridden and materialized soul of the human, corrupted in the marketplace of form, into a "virgin soul" free from the confines and prison house of duality. This purified virgin soul is now ready for the bed of union with God the eternal spouse.

On the Way to the Wedding

The long journey toward the final merger in God begins with a sense of spiritual emptiness and isolation. Even before any person is drawn to God, that person's thinking is based on a sense of duality consciousness. He or she feels completely cut off and separate from any sense of God. In many cases, the soul has lost all faith and even forgotten God altogether. Life seems meaningless, barren, and without purpose. God, if He is conceived at all, is perceived as a mere concept with no substance. For most, that power is a distant being, unreachable and unknown.

In time, as the soul matures, it begins to feel the radiation of divine love; and the conscious desire to know oneself arises spontaneously. Some people—the true lovers—are utterly discontent unless they are being drawn toward a state of union with this Being. The entire journey of love occurs in the consciousness of the lover. As souls are intrinsically of the same essence as God, they cannot remain content for long in this material realm. As the souls purify themselves of the worldly desires and temporal gains, they begin to feel the pull of Divine love from the heart of the Beloved.

Another way to present this mystical journey that encapsulates the milestones on the path is the following formula:

God's Out Pouring of Love
The Soul's Response
Attraction
Union
Unified Love

In this context, "God's Out Pouring of Love" means the radiance that emanates from the Divine Beloved, or God, or from an illumined spiritual master. To the extent that any of us partake of the radiance of God, we ourselves become radiant. This divine radiation is so powerfully attractive that, once perceived, the soul continually longs for this experience, desiring to experience it again and again. The soul is unable to forget the experience, for it is an experience of the Creator's unconditional love of us.

This radiance is initially supplied to the lover who is responsive to God, usually through a spiritual master who radiates this loving attraction continually to all corners of the globe. When exposed to this radiance, the heart of the lover is kindled into response. Response involves an acknowledgment by the lover of kinship with the spirit of radiance, and a desire to move toward the expression of this. In fact, it is the radiance of love that enlivens the lover's heart, as it purifies one's spirit.

This desire to draw closer can be understood as a kind of irresistible attraction. It draws the lover closer to the Beloved, and the power of this radiance emanating from the Beloved has all kinds of internal and exterior effects on the lover. The closer the lover comes, the more his or her consciousness is transformed. This journey of attraction has many stages within it, which have been mapped by mystics and sages throughout the ages.

The consummation of the state of attraction is union, in which the lover ceases to exist as an entity separate from the Beloved; all personal desires and characteristics are consumed as the lover merges without the slightest degree of differentiation into the eternal heart of the Beloved.

Once the lover has fully merged in the spiritual master, the spiritual master now merges the lover in God. The Sufis have referred to these stages as *fana fil Sheikh* (merger in the Master) and *fana fil Allah* (merger in God). At this point, lover and Beloved cease to exist as self-aware separate individuals; their awareness is completely centered in God. Whereas at the beginning, there was one perfectly realized being (the Beloved), there are now two, and the two join together in a perfectly unified essence. The lover who has become the Beloved also becomes a receptacle totally devoted to the expression of God's will, to being His conscious co-worker on earth.

The path toward final consummation has a number of particular characteristics; as with other steps, sages from all ages and many cultures have mapped the road. The stations of love referred to as follows are their markers on the journey. Although there are many different religions and spiritual traditions, there is a remarkable similarity in the actual experience of the lover walking this road. The inner path is a universal unchanging journey that transcends the limitations of culture, creed, religion, and time.

The Ten Stations of Love

In organizing this book around ten basic stages of divine love, I have drawn from the work of a number of great mystics and masters of both the East and the West. Foremost among them are Sant Darshan Singh Ji, Sant Kirpal Singh Ji, Sant Rajinder Singh Ji, Tulsi Sahib, Swami Ji, and Maharaj from the Sant Mat Tradition; Khawaja Nasir-al-din, Farid-uddin Attar, Al-Ghazzali, Hamid Ghazzali, Jalaluddin Rumi, Khwaja Hafez, and Ibn Arabi from the Sufi tradition; Meister Eckhart, Saint Teresa, Saint John of the Cross, and Hildegard of Bingen from the Christian tradition; Guru Nanak from the Sikh tradition; and Kabir, Shankara, Dadu Shahib, Mira Bai, Swami Ramakrishna, and many contemporary masters from the Hindu tradition.

It would be prudent to note here that the delineation of this journey into ten stations is not fixed in stone. Rather it represents significant milestones on the inner journey of love. In actuality, there may be many more stages of finer and finer degrees. Some of these have been articulated in the Sufi, Hindu, and Sant traditions. However, these particular stations define certain universal aspects of the journey toward the gnosis that, in the main, corroborate with other religious traditions. In addition, what is critical here in delineating these stages is the underlying change of consciousness that these stations represent.

It is important to remember that these stages are not intellectual concepts but spiritual states. They are therefore subjective descriptions of reality. No words fully capture them nor can they. They point to the reality but do not explain it.

These states represent unique turning points or transformations. From a practical point of view, each one poses certain immediate and direct challenges to the lover. As each soul is unique, each soul's responses will likewise contain different subjective elements. To move to the next stage, the lover must master the lessons of love at this level. In general, the stages can be organized around the unifying principles of separation and union, and the dissolving of the lover's identity as a separate and distinct entity. In this context, the word "identity" means the lover's consciousness of his or her illusory personality or egoic self. The real identify of all souls is not separate from or different from our Source—God. That ultimate identify is Love itself.

The Honeymoon of Divine Love

Love Emanates From the Heart of the Beloved.

—Sant Darshan Singh Ji

The first station of this remarkable journey of love is referred to by esoteric Christians as the "call." It is in this period that the lover experiences the initial pangs of longing for God. During this first phase, the lover is put through a series of difficult trials and outer purifications to cleanse the lover of worldly entanglements and mindless wanderings in sense pleasures. This phase of preparatory cleansing is orchestrated by the Beloved to test the soul's depth of longing and sincerity. The Divine Beloved makes arrangements for the meeting of the guru with the disciple. "When the disciple is ready," the saying goes, "the Master appears."

This phase is one in which the soul is often confused and filled with incessant doubts. The heart is essentially still enmeshed in the world and its affairs and is easily sidetracked or diverted from its inner journey.

This stage of the lover-Beloved relationship is also characterized by an overwhelming display of personal and intimate love for the would-be lover given by a God-personified master. This desire, in due course, intensifies to such an extent that the lover's uppermost desire is to be in the physical presence of his or her Beloved. The master, who is a living reflection of God's love, responds by granting this desire in proportion to the lover's need, and receptivity.

During this initial response, God, working through the physical form of a spiritual master, often showers an overwhelming amount of personal affection upon the lover. The Beloved's radiant glances give the lover a taste of the divine oneness of love. In this rare display of personalized love, the lover rises into a state of wondrous ecstasy. The soul of the lover, by drinking deeply of the love of the Beloved, becomes drunk on this personal affection. This stage is consummated when the silken bonds of love are tied in the corridors of the heart and the lover's fate is sealed by a deep and abiding attachment to the Beloved.

During this phase, which some Sufi masters have called the honeymoon of love, the Beloved, working in the form of an illumined master, almost spoils the lover for good with personal solicitude and love-laden glances. The love of the lover, however, remains entirely exteriorized, for it has yet to experience any test of fidelity or sincerity. This next phase is sometimes referred to as *ulfa* (attachment) by the Sufis and *rati* (inner spiritual attachment) by Kabir.

It is here that the first test of love reveals the depths of the lover's true aspirations.

The Ripening of Love

The second and third station of love is primarily focused on further deepening of the lover's intimacy with the Beloved and testing the lover's sincerity and faith through interiorizing the process of love. In Sufi terminology, this stage is called *ṣadaqa* (truth), because it is here that the lover's loyalty and commitment meet their first challenges. Here the truth or sincerity of the lover's heart is tested. Hence the lover, during this stage, often meets with intense criticism and rebuke from friends, family, and society. In some cases, the lover finds himself or herself completely alone and abandoned.

In the third phase of this station, the helpless lover now encounters, to his or her immense surprise, gentle rebukes from the lips of the Beloved. The Beloved, in seeking to interiorize the lover's love, often hurls barbed jabs into the heart of the lover. The fortunate lover, however, realizes that this, too, is a gift from the Beloved and accepts these minor chastisements with newfound humility and gratitude.

After undergoing a variety of trials and tribulations at the hands of the Beloved, the lover quickly learns to examine his or her heart and discover when he or she is in error. The completion of this stage is reached when the lover is able to swim in the ocean of the Beloved's love without the boat of personal attention.

The lover, having made a complete turnaround from the privileged state of intimacy, now nourishes love through the inner remembrance of the Beloved. In the Christian mystic tradition, this is described by Saint John of the Cross as the "kindling of the living flame of love" and represents the lover's ability to nourish love with or without the Beloved's outer display of affection.

The Valley of Sincerity: The Vale of Tears

In the third stage of this remarkable journey, the lover's longing for the Beloved intensifies. As the lover now sits regularly in inner meditation, having divested himself or herself of the need for outer affection, the lover finds a gradual increase in the experience of inner radiant Light. This gradual increase of inner Light produces, in proportional measure, a restlessness and agitation that the lover has never known before. This new pain cannot be contained in the fragile heart of the lover. He or she longs for more love, but it is not to be given.

Being still raw in love, the lover bewails his or her lot and retreats into the dark corners of spiritual sorrow and contraction. This state, while it may look like depression from an outsider's perceptive, is far from depression. It is in fact a deepening of love, which further detaches the lover from all that distracts from the Beloved.

Withdrawing into the heart still further, the lover begins to shed copious tears in desperate longing for the Beloved. These tears signal the purifying process of interiorizing the lover's love. This station is completed when the lover becomes caught in the manacle of the Beloved's glances and accepts without complaint a position of servitude and dependence. Each of these tears is, in fact, a divine gift. There is no doubt that one has to clean the filth that is inside if one is to reach perfection. From the lover's eyes, even a single particle of dirt in his or her inner universe is a hundred thousand times more foul that dirt on the outside.

The lover comes to know which water washes away the inner dirt. The tears of true longing, not just any teardrops, are the teardrops from which purity of love grows. It is the innocent pure tears from a real eye that can see. These tears wash away the dirt of ages upon ages and grant security and liberation. In such a person, sleep changes, and slumber also becomes wakeful. But tears without yearning for God, meditation without longing, does not go further than the edge of our grave—meaning it does not change the inner heart.

The lover now learns that prayers made with inner intention, yearning, and true supplication enter into the heart and travel with one until one stands before God. These tears go even to Paradise and proceed with one to the most exalted station of the Truth—the true abode of Love. Such is the power of the real tears born of longing for truth.

The Valley of Separation

Movement into the fourth stage begins only after separation becomes seemingly unbearable and the predominant experience of the lover is profound agony coupled with a passionate and unceasing inner remembrance of the Beloved. This station is distinguished from the preceding one in several ways.

First, the lover remains in a state bordering on semi-death. Death, in fact, appears to the lover to be the only release from this ceaseless inner torture. The lover spends his or her nights in prolonged vigils, continues to shed copious tears, and prays for an end to this unbearable state. The lover eats little, talks little, and, in general, lessens to whatever degree is possible his or her connection with worldly pursuits. Often, however, the state of the lover is concealed from the eyes of the world because one cannot explain one's condition to those not traveling the path.

In passing through this valley of separation, the lover adds the glance of his or her own love for the Beloved to the glance of loveliness from the Beloved. In other words, the lover's longing and desperate need for the Beloved are facets of the Beloved's need for the lover's love.

The glance of the Beloved is called, in Sufi terminology, the glance of loveliness. It is a transforming experience for one who can receive the revelation it contains. It does not become the glance of belovedness, however, until the lover is emptied of self while gazing into the eyes of the Beloved or spiritual Master. The Beloved's beauty is contingent upon the recognition of that beauty by the lover. Otherwise the Beloved's beauty remains in the realm of the imagination. It is the joy of the joy of knowing how beautiful the Beloved truly is. Sant Darshan Singh beautifully articulates this amazing state:

> *As the beauty of the Beloved's eye*
> *caught the light of mine,*
> *It became even more ravishing*
> *and irresistible.*[15]

In this stage, the lover quickly matures in his or her love and realizes not only the emptiness of his or her own being, but also the grandeur of the Beloved's beauty. As long as the lover is preoccupied with the search for love, he or she does not taste of the fruits of inner union. The lover's emptying of himself or herself is the first phase of this process of separation. It then proceeds through the corridors of endurance to complete resignation. But this process of complete surrender is a slow one and accompanied by many a test and struggle along the way.

This resignation on the part of the lover allows the Beloved to handle the whole affair as He likes. In giving up the tantalizing fruit of union, the lover realizes that the agony of separation itself, in the strangest of ways, is the cure for one's own pain. The fire that once consumed one is now consumed with relish. This is the point at which the lover begins to merge with the inner Beloved or "light form" of the master.

The heart of the lover now becomes seasoned to living in a state of anguish and, strangely, even begins to enjoy the "atrocities of the Beloved." The term "atrocities" of the Beloved refers to the paradoxical state in which the lover no longer experiences the master's indifference or lack of concern as painful. Instead it becomes an inner delight, for the lover has realized that this, too, is meant to increase the lover's longing and decrease his or her limited selfish love. The lover now knows every act of the Beloved is an act of unconditional love meant to "end" attraction for anything other than the Beloved, for all desires, including the desire for union, are veils on the face of the Beloved. Sant Darshan Singh observed:

> *The blood of my desires has been shed a thousand times,*
> *But nobody has ever seen even a tear in my eye.*[16]

The Valley of Concealment

In the fifth stage of the journey, the lover enters the feast of inner radiance and subsists on the inner radiant form of the Beloved. This station is called *shaqhif* by the Sufis, and "illumination" by the esoteric Christians. During this stage, the lover is required to exhibit three distinct traits. First, he or she spontaneously carries out the commands of the Beloved without intellectual questioning. Second, the lover remains continuously alert against anything, except God, that may enter the citadel of his or her heart. Third, the lover is required to maintain absolute secrecy with regard to his or her love for the Beloved.

During this stage, the lover lives on the inner radiant showers of light and love bestowed upon him or her from within the temple of the heart. The lover's days are filled with remembrance of God, and nights are an endless round of vigils and fasts. The only hope lies in pleasing the Beloved. Though the lover may desire the darshan of the spiritual master, he or she knows that both union and separation are in the hands of the Beloved and worries only about being able to serve and obey Him. The lover continues to immerse himself or herself in the service of the Beloved, missing not a single opportunity to help others. Here the fountains of divine compassion begin to flow, and love of all creation effortlessly flows from the lover's being.

The Valley of Estrangement

In the sixth station, which some Sufis have called "exclusive attachment," the lover turns from himself or herself, the world, and all things that are "other." This includes even the Beloved. As the lover breaks the idols of "otherness," the ecstatic vision of the Beloved becomes more steady and prolonged within the lotus of his or her heart. In this stage, the first pages of the book of ecstasy are opened and the lover begins to live in near continuous bliss, even in the midst of all activities.

As this bliss deepens, it becomes part and parcel of every atom of the lover's body, radiating peace and joy to all. From this overflowing joy, a spiritual certitude and trust emerge. Here the lover knows how little he or she knows and this emptiness is itself a great mystery. Every moment, the lover seeks to offer himself or herself at the altar of the Beloved. With every passing moment, he or she offers a thousand hearts, giving away everything he or she is, to secure the divine Beloved.

The Valley of Unity

During the seventh station, the lover becomes unmoved by any outer disgrace, blame, poverty, or other condition. What was once material now becomes immaterial and insignificant. The chains of the world are broken and the lover feels infinitely freer and indifferent to any personal sufferings that may pass through. The Beloved responds by perfecting the lover's conduct in the world and opens up the book of creation to him or her. The lover steps into the infinite palace of knowledge and becomes a person of true insight.

In this field of unity, the lover's actions in the world of forms exhibit perfect serenity and he or she acts without the least bit of personal desire. The lover pays homage to the Divine Beloved, now witnessed in every atom, in every leaf, and in every shining petal. Having reached the door of the Beloved, the lover's ardor for complete and final union knows no limits. Standing and gazing at the glory of the Beloved, the lover steps unabashedly into a sea of ecstasy and intoxication.

The Valley of Ecstasy

During the eighth station, called ecstasy, or *wajud* by the Sufis, the lover takes the plunge into the sea of intoxication and loses his or her reason and senses. During this precarious stage, the lover resembles a madman who runs wildly hither and thither in search of the Beloved. Overwhelmed by this ocean of intoxication, the lover converses with the trees and the stones, in the mad ecstasy of love. Here the inner worlds illuminate the way and every cry for help is met by a thousand shafts of light. The lover's whole being has become a polished mirror reflecting and radiating the Light of the Beloved's love. The great Sufi saint Al Yafi'i gives us a hint of this state:

> *They say: Thou art become mad with love for thy Beloved.*
> *I reply: The savior of life is for madmen.*[17]

The Valley of Bewilderment

The ninth station has been called "astonishment and bewilderment" by the Sufis and "death in Christ" by esoteric Christians. In this stage, the lover experiences the most brutal of sorrows and humiliations. The very ground upon which he or she walks appears to be a mirage, and the seven heavens and all the universes appear as dust before the supremacy of his or her love. The lover can find no resting place within or without.

Ironically, although the lover is encamped in the tavern of unity, he or she has still not entered the bed of the Beloved. Here the lover knows nothing of himself or herself, and weeps for a Beloved about whom he or she knows nothing. In this stage, the lover experiences complete isolation from everything material. There is not even the slightest thread of connection to the ephemeral passing existence of life. In this state, the physical, subtle (astral), and causal universes disappear; there is neither eternity nor non-eternity, neither existence nor nonexistence. Here, life has no meaning outside the "tresses of the Beloved." The great mystic and martyr of love Al-Hallaj said:

I am he whom I love and he whom I love is I,
We are two spirits dwelling in one body.
If thou seeth me thou seeth Him.
If thou seeth Him thou seeth us both.[18]

Or in the words of Saint John, "I have been crucified with Christ. It is no longer I who live, but Christ who lives in me" (Gal. 2:20 ESV). The lover at this point is quite willing to give up his or her entire life if it means meeting the Beloved. For there is no concern any longer for one's own life. Sant Darshan Singh spoke beautifully of this wondrous state:

O men of lust, beware of entering
    this lane of love,
Here you will find only
    the cross and the gallows.[19]

The Valley of Unending Oneness

The tenth and final stage enumerated by the Sufi Chiragh-i-Delhi is that of complete merger in the Beloved. At this stage, the lover is beset by tremendous dangers and obstacles. Here the full force of unthinkable suffering falls upon the head of the one who makes this journey. This state is characterized by total negation of the lover on the part of the Beloved and total helplessness on the part of the lover. In this rarefied atmosphere, the separate existence of the Lover ceases as an independent reality. Love, lover, and Beloved have become one essence. The drop has merged with the ocean and has become the ocean. The separate ray has become the sun.

The great Sufi saint Ibn Arabi beautifully describes the final stages of this last journey. Here the creed of the lover is only intoxication, and it is an intoxication that leads to complete eradication of the lover's ego. From this state of egolessness, the lover experiences absence from himself or herself and all objective reality. The lover is then further crushed by the complete shattering forever of the ego and sense of his or her reality. Here the subtle casual seeds of individual separateness are scattered as dust in the winds of divine union. The lover no longer has even a thin vein between himself or herself and the ultimate Reality. Here the lover's separate existence is totally annihilated and then lost even to the knowledge of this annihilation. By this is meant the lover no longer has a sense of his or her own attainment, and even the memory of this distinction is also eradicated. Here the lover exists only in name. To quote one great Sufi: "Love is the negation of all the attributes of the lover and the positioning of the Beloved Himself in their place."[20]

From this Eternal Fount of Oneness, an unending stream of love flows forth. Although each of these ten states is unique and poses a particular challenge or test, certain stages may appear to overlap or to take place simultaneously. One of the problems of presenting a book organized into such sections is that the description of each stage makes it seem somehow detached from the preceding and subsequent stage. For the lover, however, these experiences appear to flow fluidly from one stage to another, and sudden catalytic moments occur only rarely.

States and Stages on the Journey

It is also important to note that the experience of these various states—of longing, trust, faith, certitude, ecstasy, and so on—is present at all stages of the journey to one degree or another. The changes in stage are identified by the degree to which a particular state is experienced, and in the way it affects the lover's understanding of himself or herself.

Thus, there may be many moments of ecstasy during the journey, even in the initial stages, but these are not to be confused with the stage in which ecstasy is not a passing phase but the predominant inner dynamic of the lover's reality. The Sufis have articulated this difference by the use of two terms: *hal* and *maqam*. Hal is usually a state which comes suddenly and then passes, giving immediate insight and a certain knowledge or epiphany. But this state does not last long and may fade within days; if integrated, however, this state may lead to higher, more lasting states. Maqam is a stage that has been attained through long struggle and tribulation and, once attained, is usually not lost. The ten stages represent ten maqams along the way. The various distinctions in each state depend upon the lover's ability to open completely to each teaching moment.

The great Rumi gives us a visual and poetic explanation of this subtle difference: "The state of hal is like the unveiling of that beauteous bride, while maqam station is the being alone with the bride."[21] Though at times these states are difficult to articulate clearly, their existence is an esoteric fact to those who have traveled the path of divine love. The Qur'an states (Surah 6: Cattle: Section 10, 83–90):

We raise whom We will, degree after degree:
for thy Lord is full of wisdom and knowledge.

These subjective descriptions are not meant to represent absolute reality, which is beyond states of limited subjective vision. These states and stages represent subtle subjective experiences beyond the range of normal psychological states. They function as signposts along the way, indicating to the lover his or her degree of nearness to Truth. Just as our vision of objective reality depends upon our visual acumen, point of view, and emotional states, so, too, does the vision of Truth depend upon the subjective state through which the wayfarer is passing. These ten unique stations are meant to provide wayfarers with certain knowledge and vision necessary to move forward.

Understanding the process prepares the lover to recognize the challenge of the moment. Awareness of the significance of the moment is the precondition upon which appropriate response is built. If there is no awareness, the moment passes, and the perfection of the moment is lost. If the moment is lost, it must be repeated until mastery is attained. In the supreme game of love, only a perfect lover becomes a Perfect Beloved.

Chapter Two
The Call: Love Emanates from the Heart of the Beloved

God became man that man might become God.

—Saint Athanasius, Saint Augustine, Saint Cyril of Alexandria, Meister Eckhart, Guru Nanak, Jacob Boehme, Rumi, Kirpal Singh, Attar, Hafiz, Rama Krishna, Hazur Baba Sawan Singh, Sai Baba, Christ, and many others[1]

Almost all spiritual traditions have laid great stress on the need for a guide or teacher on the spiritual journey. The very first stage of the journey to God involves the lover in a direct relationship with the guide or spiritual master. Sant Kirpal Singh Ji Maharaj has stated this quite forcefully:

> It is the Master's grace that can pull a spirit out of the physical sheath right above the plane of the senses, enabling her to move unfettered to higher spiritual visions and attain her native Godhead. Without a Master, it is sheer darkness, and one sinks into bottomless depths.[2]

Swami Ramdas (1886–1963) went so far as to say, "Even God cannot grant *moksha* [deliverance] but only the guru."[3] This seeming overstatement is justified, for the spiritual guide or *rasul* (Arabic: intercessor) is the very means God has designed for the soul's liberation. Mysticism, then, begins with a soulful invitation by the teacher, to enter into the lover-Beloved relationship.

In the Christian scriptures, John tells us, "You did not choose me, but I chose you and appointed you that you should go and bear fruit…" (John 15:16 ESV). In Christian terms, it is Christ who first loves us. Our love is only reciprocal. John tells us again, "We love because he first loved us" (John 4:19 ESV).

It is the God-man, the guru, the Christ power, who initiates our love for Him, without which there would be no relationship at all. It is through the God-man that the power of God acts and moves. Masters are living representatives of God. They have developed all the qualities of God. Though their bodies are made of physical matter, they are windows to the infinite. They are the Logos made flesh.

The first stage of this relationship of the lover to spiritual master or guide begins when the lover feels an inner pull to live in close proximity to a spiritual master. During this stage, the lover, moved by the grace apparent in the initial gift, seeks the door of a guide or master. In mystic literature, love is always depicted as emanating from the heart of the Beloved. It is this love from a God-man that fires the lover into desiring to be as close as possible to a spiritual master.

In the Old Testament, this point is alluded to in the book of Ecclesiastes (6:36):

> *If thou see a man of understanding,*
> *go to him early in the morning*
> *and let thy foot wear the steps of his doors.*

In his initiation in the wilderness, Abraham was blessed by Melchizidek, King of Salem. There are similar examples throughout the scriptures confirming the fact that without contact with a guide or master, spirituality is unrealizable.

Some masters have gone so far as to insist that those who are not under the guidance of a competent master are under the guidance of Satan, the master of the material world. Bayazid al-Bistami, the great Sufi master known for his miraculous powers, once said, "The guide of those who have no guide is satan."[4] Jesus Christ said, "Whoever is not with me is against me, and whoever does not gath-

er with me scatters" (Matt. 12:30 ESV). Jesus describes the role of
the God-man in the simplest of language (Matt. 11:27 ESV):

*All things have been handed over to me by my Father, and no one
knows the Son except the Father, and no one knows the Father
except the Son and anyone to whom the Son chooses to reveal him.*

Sant Kirpal Singh similarly supports this role of the God-man:
"God is unchangeable and everlasting permanence. But we have
not yet seen Him. So we have, of necessity, to bestow our loving
devotion on the human pole where the God is manifest." Guru
Amardas Ji, the third guru of the Sikhs, says, "If you want to
worship God, worship the Satguru, who is God personified or the
word made flesh."[5]

The belief that the spiritual journey can be successfully completed without the aid of some master soul has never been advo-
cated by the great spiritual masters. Rumi reminds us in his poetic
tongue:

*The fleshly soul is a dragon
with hundred-fold strength and cunning:
the face of the Shaykh [Master]
is the emerald that plucks out its eye.*[6]

Many wonderful words have been written about the greatness
of the master souls and the wondrous things that happen in their
presence. Simply being in their company charges the disciple with
profound spiritual uplift. Sant Kirpal Singh expresses this point
clearly:

*Masters are the overflowing cups of the Lord's intoxicating color —
overflowing vessels of love. Just by enjoying His company the
yearning for God is born within one's being. He creates love, for He
is all love, He teaches how to love — the rays of love issue forth from
Him wherever He goes. His words are uttered to increase the love
within us.*[7]

The entire edifice of love is predicated and built upon the relationship between the teacher and the disciple.

This profoundly important connection with the teacher is established initially through the gift of initiation. Moinuddin Chisti, a Sufi sage, has stated, "Those beings who have reached that illuminated state of perfection have the ability to enlighten the hearts of the people with divine light."[8] Speaking of this priceless gift, Swami Sivananda, a modern Indian saint, described the process of initiation as the "direct link with the divine being."[9]

The Master as Expert

Although the tradition of the living master has been customary in Sufi, Hindu, Buddhist, Jain, and Sikh traditions, there is ample evidence in Christianity, Judaism, and Taoism to support the need for a living guide capable of direct spiritual transmission. Thomas Norton, a renowned English alchemist of the fourteenth century, spoke of the master or teacher as One divinely sent by God to instruct the disciple so that he or she may be taught from "mouth to mouth."[10]

Chang Po-tuan, familiar with the secret oral teachings of Chinese alchemy, also warned against "constrained conjecture" and the inability to "succeed unless you have a true teacher."[11] In reality, as an authentic master is merged in God, there is little or no difference between His inner being and God Himself. But we must remember the outer form of the master is not the God-power or true master.

This realization, however, is hardly imaginable during the beginnings of this relationship. A novice can seldom recognize a true master, even if he or she is face to face with such a being. This apparent paradox is also part of the divine plan, for the master reveals himself in accordance with the degree of spiritual maturity of the lover. How could a primary school student have any idea of the depth of knowledge of a college professor?

Likewise the *qutub*, or spiritual pole, as the Sufis have called it, reveals himself as the soul ascends into the higher planes of consciousness. He becomes the vehicle through which the lover experiences God's love. The teacher is the perfection of God's manifestation of love in time and space. Universal Man is more than the bringer of spiritual redemption cosmically and personally; such a being is the prototype of God on earth. God is indeed manifest in the guru, as the guru is manifest in all. Jesus Christ proclaimed that his authority was, indeed, God's authority (Matt. 28:18 ESV):

> *Then Jesus came to them and said, "All authority in heaven and on earth has been given to me."*

We in the West are often averse to seeing the need for a living spiritual master. Yet in every other field of endeavor, we are hesitant to proceed without a teacher. We would shun a doctor or lawyer who had not taken the appropriate studies at an accredited institution with experts in the field. The refusal, in our culture, to accept a spiritual authority reflects our society's disregard for tradition. Sawan Singh, the great sage of Beas, once remarked:

> *There is no contention about the clouds dispensing the rain. No one expects the rain to come out of the clear blue sky. Why then should not the perfect guide or mentor distribute the rain of His mercy and grace?*[12]

Sri Ramana Maharshi, the renowned nondualist sage of India, stated the same theme in his own idiom: "God and guru are not really different; they are identical."[13] By knowing the one, the disciple knows the other. Again Jesus tells us: "If ye had known me, ye should have known my Father also: and from henceforth ye know him, and have seen him" (John 14:7 KJV). The guru who truly fulfills the role of "dispeller of darkness" is an inseparable ingredient on the spiritual path. It is the guru whose company provides "the keys which unlock the doors of Paradise," as Attar so rightly noted.

Drawn by the Spiritual Master

An ironic twist of fate is that it is not the disciple who finds the teacher, but the master who first loves the disciple and draws him or her to the master's feet. Bayazid al Bastami, a great Sufi master of Persia, spoke of this strange paradox:

For a long time I was under the delusion that I loved Him. But the truth is that it was He who first loved me.[14]

This somewhat strange reversal of roles is one of the great mysteries of the spiritual path. At the heart of this paradox is the notion that love is a gift of the Beloved and brings the disciple from selfishness to selflessness and from separation unto union. Kabir, the great sixteenth-century Indian poet and master, describes the condition of one who has realized this in his or her heart:

Kabir says to go and get the company of some saint.
Keep the company of Him who has controlled His mind.
Without measure will He give the wealth of Naam or love.
Shun the company of the worldly
Who may give you milk and honey.
I ask not for powers miraculous,
Kabir says, "Give me the Master's Darshan [company] daily."[15]

Kabir's instructions may appear almost naive at first glance. Yet out of thousands of disciples who start the journey, only a rare few come to see the full significance of the God-man. A number of spiritual traditions even state that the existence of the entire universe is predicated upon the presence of some perfect being in its midst. In the Jewish faith, we find a similar notion in the concept of the thirty-six *Zadikim* (perfect ones), without whose support the world would collapse. So, too, in the Sufi tradition, the Qutub is the cohesive glue that cements the world together.

The human being was created for the sole purpose of knowing and worshiping God. The realization of this divine light, love, and life in each of us was the reason for which the world was created, and without their manifest presence, existence has no purpose. The God-man represents the prototypical perfection that lies latent in each of us. Without the masters' light shining in the vastness of this material darkness, the world would cease to exist. A God-intoxicated devotee tells us:

> *O Thou, the light of whose beauty has*
> *Illuminated the beauties of this world.*
> *The reflection of thy excellence has fallen on them.*
> *Everywhere are found the manifestations of thy beauty.*
> *In everyone is found the passion of thy love.*[16]

After hearing about these great beings of love, it is natural that the would-be lover develops an interest in meeting and spending time in the company of one of them. Jesus said, "My sheep hear my voice, and I know them, and they follow me" (John 10:27 ESV). Coming to the holy feet of a master is not an accidental occurrence. It is the result of the master's specific love for the human concerned. It is a rare soul that, after lifetimes of long and arduous struggle, comes into the fold of a perfect saint. To enter into the orbit of a master soul is God's most precious gift, the full significance of which is never fully known by the lover. It may appear that the disciple finds the master, but, as noted, it is the master who draws the disciple to him.

Ascended and Past Masters

Although most spiritual traditions acknowledge the role of a living spiritual guide, the cry of the soul never goes unheeded. The supreme power of love works in myriad ways, carefully tending to the evolution of each and every spark of divine Light, no matter what form it may embody. Every soul, regardless of its life form, is on its evolutionary journey home. Though it is possible to contact past masters for spiritual guidance, many esoteric texts confirm that it is unwise to rely solely on such sources, as direct revelation usually occurs only for a small minority of evolved souls.

In addition, ascended masters usually choose to work through, and in cooperation with, the spiritual luminaries of the day. In this way, an unbroken transmission of light and power can be maintained across many generations. Finally, ascended masters and adepts generally focus their guidance on those souls on the inner planes who require further assistance. Like a commander in the field, the living spiritual guide is in a unique position to perceive and address the innumerable difficulties and needs that arise in the course of a disciple's journey.

Trial and Sacrifice

For most of us, the thirst for spiritual revelation involves much searching and, often, great suffering and anguish. Every scripture portrays this "valley of the shadow of death" as an experience of deep soul searching. This is the experience of the "dark night of the soul" in which the soul undergoes drastic and traumatic purification as it is prepared for its unveiling before the divine bride.

This apparent suffering is a prerequisite for the encounter with the Beloved. But suffering is not undergone for its own sake; it exists only to prepare the soul for its heavenly journey. Just as the word "sacrifice" essentially means make "sacred," so, too, suffering is a sort of interior fire, a *tapas*, as the Hindus call it, which removes the contingent from essence. In this stage, the sincere faith of the lover is tested because, without trial or sacrifice, the eyes of the bird of the soul remain fixed upon the carrion of the material world instead of the pearl of the Beloved's eye. This stage may be long or short depending upon the degree of sincerity and depth of yearning in each soul.

The consummation of this stage is accomplished when the lover arrives at the doorstep of the Beloved and is lucky enough to realize, in the words of Saint Alphonsus Liguori, a seventeenth-century Benedictine mystic:

How often has it happened that what we consider
a punishment and chastisement of God,
was a special work of grace,
an act of His infinite mercy.[17]

Following Page:

The Pure Land
Musée Guimet, Paris

This eighteenth-century Japanese illustration depicts the palace of Sakhavati. The palace, the Western Paradise of the Mahayana Buddhist sect, is rich with gold and gems. These are symbolic of the manifested light and beauty of this realm. Entry into this paradise is achieved only after passing through the fire of separation and subduing the hydra-headed serpent of desire. Yet, for the true lover, the delights of heaven become insipid in comparison to the majesty and glory of the Divine Beloved.

Chapter Three
The Valley of Intimacy: The Development of Remembrance

Your remembrance is sewn to the hem of my heart;
No matter where I go, I cannot forget my sorrow.
— Darshan Singh

And I will bring forth in shining light those who have loved My holy name,
and I will seat each on the throne of his honor.
— The Book of Enoch, CVIII V 12

Initiation: The Path of Discipleship

In the preceding stage, we saw how the spiritual guide becomes the embodiment of the lover's ideal and is, in fact, responsible for the first flickering of love that begins to smolder in the lover's heart. It is usually at this critical juncture that the disciple enters into a formal bond of spiritual fellowship, known in most sacred traditions as "initiation." The subject of initiation is complex and involved, and this chapter covers only its most important features as they relate to the development of the lover-Beloved relationship.

On its most literal level, initiation represents a formal acceptance by a teacher of a student into a specific spiritual order. Although each spiritual order differs in outer rituals, the essence of initiation is the direct transmission of the life impulse of the spiritual master into the disciple. True spiritual initiation goes far beyond common practices such as being given a certain mantra, receiving a new name, or being accepted into a church or congregation. The bestowal of this life impulse involves a firsthand, direct experience of the inner celestial Light and rapturous divine Music. Such inner experiences form the basis of the inner mystical bond that connects the master to his disciple. Almost all religious traditions refer to this direct inner experience.

Throughout the ages, this ever-living current of Light and Sound has gone by many names. In the Zoroastrian scriptures, it is *Sraosha* (incarnate Word) and *Anaghra Raochah* (Endless Celestial Light); in the Greek and Hellenistic worlds, it was the music of the spheres (*musica universalis*) of Pythagoras, and the *Logos* (Word) of Heraclites. In the Abrahamic traditions, in the Jewish Torah in the book of *Bereshith*/Genesis, God said, "Let there be Light" (Aur). From this emanated the *Aur Ein Sof* (Infinite Limitless Light). In Christianity, Christ is the *phos alethinon* (true light) and Jesus is the *logos sarx* (Word made flesh). In Islam, there is *Nur illahi* or Light of God in the Qur'an and the Light of Lights (*Nur al-anwar*) of Suhrawardi, as well as the *Kalma i-Qadeem* (unfathomable Ancient Word).

Moving east, the Vedas teach that *Purusha* (Absolute Self) is *jyotirmay purusha* (made of light) and *jyotir uttamam* (supreme light). The Vedic universe springs forth from *naad* (vibration) or *vak* (Word), and is followed in the Bhagavad Gita, where we find *brahma-tejas* (the effulgence of the absolute). The Buddha speaks of the brightly shining mind (Pāli: *pabhassara citta*) and clear light of awareness (Tibetan: *Ösel;* Sanskrit: *prabhasvara*) that resides as the *bhavanga* (Pāli: "ground of being"). The Sikh and Sant Mat traditions, which share a common vocabulary, call us to hearken to the *anahad shabd* (unstruck melody), *naam* (creative vibration), *bani* (divine song), and *jyoti* (light).

The essence of initiation is the direct transmission of the spiritual power of the Master into the heart of the disciple. The details of this experience vary from person to person, but they represent an unbreakable bond of spiritual love, grace, and guidance between the master and the disciple.

The full nature of this relationship is impossible to understand from the outside. The commitment on the part of the master is a profound one, for the master assumes the full weight of responsibility for the ultimate evolution of that soul. The nature of this responsibility is itself a grand mystery, and reveals itself only as the disciple matures in love and receptivity.

Initiation may be performed in a variety of ways. A formal initiation ceremony is no indication of whether one has received such a transmission. Sant Rajinder Singh tells us that a truly competent saint can convey such a transmission through a glance or a gesture, or even from thousands of miles away. The perfect saint, in fact, is not constrained by time or space and can unleash the floodgates of grace to whomsoever he or she chooses, at any time.

In the past, according to Kabir, initiation was generally given only after a disciple had spent months or even years in the company of such an enlightened being. In the closing years of the twentieth century, few, if any, have time to spend years in the company of a saint. In past ages, much inner work was required before a soul was deemed worthy of initiation. As the floodgates of grace open more fully in this new millennium, the gift of initiation is frequently given and the disciple is then asked to continue the work of inner purification subsequently.

During this stage of the journey, the would-be lover knows little of the true greatness of the Beloved and, though desirous of embarking upon this great quest, has little knowledge of the many obstacles and inner torture that lie ahead of him or her. If our wayfarer is fortunate, he or she meets a true guide and receives the priceless gift of Inner Divine Light and Sound. It is in this first experience that the lover gets a taste of the feast of unconditional love that lies in his or her destiny.

The formal or informal acceptance of a disciple into the spiritual bond with a competent master, through the process of initiation, is a prerequisite for the passage into the second phase of this stage, which I have called intimacy. In *The Cloud of Unknowing,* a classic work on Christian contemplation by an unknown medieval author who well knew the potent forces that begin to stir in the heart of the disciple, the second phase is referred to as "the blind stirring of love."

The Sufis of the school of Moinuddin Chisti have called it *sadaqa,* literally, "truth." I have thought it better to apply the word "sincerity" to its translation because this is, in fact, a phase in which one's loyalty and sincerity are severely tested.

Living in Close Proximity

The preliminary experience of this phase of intimacy is, as noted earlier, a direct result of the Beloved's own love, which has been injected into the heart of the disciple. Later, as the seed of this love begins to grow, an overwhelming desire to live in close proximity to the Beloved seizes the lover's mind. In due course, this results in the meeting of the lover with the spiritual master/Beloved, and time is spent in the court of the Beloved's graciousness.

During this period, the lover generally loses his or her wits around the Beloved and is in simultaneous awe and fear of the Beloved. Every detail, every word, even the way the Beloved dresses and ties his or her shoes evokes awe and wonderment in the lover's heart. In the Jewish tradition, it is said that a certain disciple was asked why he had come to study at the feet of the great Bal Shem Tov (Master of the Name). He replied, "To learn how he ties his shoes."

The lover's fascination with every aspect of the Beloved's life develops an intimate inner dialogue of soul to soul and heart to heart. The time spent during these days is the most treasured of all moments in the lover's life. During this phase, the Beloved showers seemingly limitless torrents of ecstasy upon the lover. The lover, in turn, nearly drowns in the sea of personal affection bestowed upon him or her.

These rare displays of personal intimacy, however, soon lay a trap for the lover, who now becomes enmeshed in what the Sufis have called "the shackles of the Beloved's love." The poor lover, while enjoying the seemingly unending fiesta of the Beloved's lyrical glances, now begins to question his or her worthiness to receive them. From this moment on, the lover is slowly yet decisively made aware of his or her own shortcomings while the majesty of the Beloved steadily grows and grows.

In this way, the lover is fashioned and molded by the Beloved's direct display of love. Gradually, this dependency of the lover on the Beloved is increased to such an extent that the lover can barely tolerate living apart from the Beloved's company. As it is usually not in the hand of fortune for the lover always to be in the physical presence of the Beloved, the lover becomes distraught and anxious.

In due course, the lover's heart ripens and tears flow in sorrowful pleas to be in the physical presence of the Beloved. If this phase matures, the Beloved usually tests the sincerity of the lover's cries by creating significant hardships and obstacles to the fulfillment of the lover's desire. It is not unusual at this stage for the lover to undergo many kinds of tribulation in order to catch a mere passing glance from the cherished Beloved. Hafiz remarks on this state of separation, characterized by the humbleness and constant entreaty that envelops the lover:

True, that I am separated from thee.
I pray that none may feel this agony.
Still I hope that soon I will be with thee.[1]

In a similar passage in the Adi Granth, the sacred scriptures of the Sikhs, the poet remarks:

Without my Beloved I have no comfort
and I am weeping all alone. O Nanak, a wife
who does not meet her husband is miserable.

The story of Leila and Majnun wonderfully illustrates the condition of the lover enmeshed in the "shackles of love." Majnun greatly adored Leila, his beloved. One day a man who lived near Majnun saw him sifting the earth by the road and said, "Majnun, what are you looking for?"

"I am looking for Leila," he replied.

The man asked, "Do you hope to find Leila there?"

"I look for her everywhere," said Majnun, "in the hope of finding her somewhere."

So, too, is the attitude of the true lover caught up in the spirit of the quest. After receiving the first draft of wine from the flagon of the Beloved's eyes, nothing matters except the pursuit of the lover's true aim. Attar described this state in these words:

Then he (the lover) will no longer fear the dragons, the
guardians of the tenth door, which seek to devour him.
When the door is opened and he enters,
then dogma, belief and unbelief all cease to exist.[2]

It is at this juncture that the dialectical nature of the lover's relationship, which is to characterize much of the subsequent journey, is first established. On the one hand, it is the lover who is seeking the Beloved, but in reality his or her love is merely a reflection of the "life-inspiring glances" of the Beloved. Though both share the same ontological reality as "essences of love," the lover is doomed to a role of separation, abandonment, rejection, hopelessness, and poverty of spirit, while the Beloved is constantly increasing in grandeur, omnipotence, glorification, and indifference.

Although they appear to contradict each other, they are, in fact, perfect mirrors of each other. The Beloved can only increase in beauty as the lover humbles himself or herself further. The seeming glory of the Beloved is no doubt perfect in itself but cannot be realized in time and space without the appearance of the lover. The full mystery of this exchange is, however, a great secret, which is dealt with more specifically later in the book.

Telling the World

During the beginning phase of this stage of intimacy, the lover, after experiencing something of the state of yearning, often expresses a newfound affection by speaking about the Beloved to every passerby. There is a well-known saying in mysticism that "He who loves a thing, speaks of it often." It is but natural in this state for the lover to express verbally what is uppermost in his or her mind. In due course, the thread of remembrance is stitched between the lover and the Beloved, and the tapestry of their love is knitted in reciprocal knots of yearning and remembrance.

These are experienced in spurts at first and naturally so, for the lover has yet to be tested in his or her love. During these initial moments of heightened receptivity, the lover will receive direct inner transmissions from the Beloved. Though these moments of ecstasy and inner attunement are brief, they will prove to be a seductive bait to lure the lover ever deeper into the heart of the Beloved. As this process continues, the lover begins to open his or her heart ever wider to the elevating and blissful dialogue with the Beloved.

Although it is well known that Jesus' disciples spread Christianity throughout the known world within just a few centuries of His ascension, it is not widely realized that the master had them go on a much earlier round of preaching. Right after He had called them, at the very beginning of their three-year lover-Beloved relationship, He had them go out to "preach the good news" to all the towns in the area. Jesus was apparently well acquainted with the lover's need, very early in the process, to tell the world about the love that has dawned in his or her heart.

The Bonds of Fellowship

This second phase of intimacy reaches its maturation when two distinct movements occur. First, and of immediate importance, is the newfound bond of fellowship that the lover recognizes with his or her co-wayfarers. This is a direct result of the Beloved's living example of reciprocity and compassion, which pours forth effortlessly and in seemingly limitless measure.

The lover no longer relates to others as one entrenched in the confines of religious dogma, but opens his or her heart in spiritual brotherhood to all souls, whatever their faith or stage of inner development. Here there is no room for pretentious devotion that elevates one religion above another or sacrifices the integrity of any living being. In the Sikh scriptures, this truth is most poignantly captured:

> *This possessiveness has gone,*
> *Since I got the radiation of the Master's company.*
> *There is no enemy, no stranger,*
> *All are now very dear to me.*[3]

Wonder and Awe

The third phase of this station is characterized by a sense of wonder and awe, which dazzles and inebriates the lover. Having tasted the divine nectar of love pouring forth from the Beloved eyes and face, the lover cannot fail to be wonder-struck. Bhai Nandlal Goya, a disciple of Guru Gobind Singh, has tried to give us some indication of this condition. He says:

> *Just to see Thy face again I once more took this physical form;*
> *otherwise what is there in this world for me; I have no interest in it.*
> *Those years are the best of my life which are spent in remembrance*

of Thee. Otherwise what was the use of my coming beneath this blue sky? What is there in the world for me? O Satguru when I forget Thee, those moments are like death.[4]

In due course, the disciple, by repeating the master's name, or by lovingly remembering him, will "get intoxication, ecstasy and joy. Our hearts will dance at the very thought of Him."[5] As the remembrance of the lover increases, he or she witnesses all beauty and majesty personified in the being of the Beloved. One poet artfully explained this predicament:

Thou art the king of the realm of beauty,
I am a helpless beggar.
My life which is not my own has no asset
except its sense of wonder.[6]

This quality of wonder arises directly from the divine bounty and fills the lover not only with the awe of the Beloved, but with a sense of his or her own nothingness as well. The paradox of this state, which is a continuous process, is the emptying of the cup of "I" ness while being immersed in the Beloved omnipresent presence.

Maria Vela, a little-known seventeenth-century Spanish mystic, overwhelmed once by her own nothingness, and deep in ecstatic prayer, seemed to hear Christ speak these comforting words: "This nothingness which you see yourself to be is what I love in you. From this nothingness you will ascend to the heights."[7]

Saint John the Baptist seems to have had a similar insight when face to face with his Divine Beloved. He said, "He must increase, but I must decrease" (John 3:30 ESV).

The German mystic and theologian Meister Eckhart captured the paradox of this state when he said, "When she has reached her limit of endeavor then will as such is free to leap over to that gnosis which is God himself. A somersault that lands the soul at the summit of her power."[8] The sense of wonder and awe the soul feels at this turning point is described in a koan by Lin Yutang:

> *First we look at the hills in the painting,*
> *Then we look at the painting in the hills.*[9]

For the lover, the boundaries of perception begin to change. What the lover sees is not what he or she perceived before. For the lover has put on the "lens of love." As love increases, the lover must decrease. In the Tao Te Ching (XLVIII), we have a remarkably similar passage that cannot help bring to mind how closely related these experiences must be:

> *He who pursues learning will increase every day;*
> *He who pursues the Tao will decrease every day.*
> *He will decrease and continue to decrease,*
> *Till he or she comes at non-action;*
> *By non-action everything can be done.*

Divine majesty is a recognizable feature of the landscape of this journey at this stage, and anyone who tastes of that abundance must find himself or herself emptied of the smallness of his or her separate self. The Greek word *metanoia*, translated in the Christian Bible as "repentance," literally means "turning away," but strongly implies "turning inward" as well. To be filled with divine presence implies the emptiness of the self; one must replace the other if the duality of illusion is to be transcended. This involves a repentance of fear and a turning inward toward God's glory and beauty.

Hujiwiri notes the difference between the repentance based upon fear caused by God's majesty versus the repentance of shame caused by the vision of God's beauty.[10] In this context, it is the repentance based upon God's beauty (*teschubah*, in Judaism) that is the true healer and our true redeemer, and it "reaches to the throne of Glory" (Talmud).

The thread of remembrance gives the lover a look at the very tapestry of divine revelation. The name and the named are interwoven, like woof and warp. With every thread of remembrance the lover weaves, the magnificent tapestry of union grows. The encounter with the Beloved is the raison d'être for the lover. Sant Darshan Singh speaks of this wondrous encounter with the zest of one who knows its depths:

> *I could neither find smiles in the flowers,*
> > *nor Light in the stars,*
> *Until I met you, O Beloved,*
> > *joy was nowhere to be found.*[11]

What magic it is to behold the face of the Beloved, and what lover would not be enthralled by the springtime-producing smile of the Beloved? Indeed, the bewitching beauty of the Beloved is all too much for the lover to bear and even a momentary glimpse of the face of the Beloved leaves the lover wonder-struck, gasping for breath and life. In this perplexing condition, the madcap lover remains a mere string of memories, which the Beloved plucks and with which He plays havoc.

In the court of love of the lover's heart, it is beauty that presides, and the entire universe is revealed to be a playground for the sport of lovemaking. Edward Young in his poem "Night Thoughts" captured this idea:

> *To reach creation; read its mighty plan*
> *In the bare bosom of the Deity.*
> *The plan and execution, to collide*
> *To see before each glance of piercing thought*
> *All cloud, all shadow, blown remote and leave.*
> *No Mystery: but that of love divine.*

Remembrance

The last phase of the journey of intimacy ends with the development of inner recollection. This intense inner remembrance of the Beloved is one of the profound turning points in the spiritual journey. Gratitude, faith, awe, and humility all flow unimpeded from the font of recollection and invocation. There is a pretemporal connection between the name and the named. The former is the essence and the latter its attributes in the world of time and space.

In the realm of time, the name of the Beloved is the connecting link to the Beloved. The repetition of any name of God produces in its wake a certain measure of closeness. By inwardly repeating the names of the Beloved, the lover invokes not only the spirit of prayer and supplication, but the very essence of that inner presence as well. The outer word purifies and cleanses the receptacle of the lover's heart until the inner essence of love, which is "the true light," manifests itself.

There may be a thousand names of God, and each religion has its own unique manner in which the Divine Beloved is addressed. But in all cases, it is the supreme nameless and formless Being who receives those calls and responds accordingly, no matter which religion or faith the lover professes. The very act of invoking the name of the Beloved establishes sympathetic bonds of communication between the one and the many.

In Eastern Orthodox Christianity, which has gained greater popularity in recent years, the initiate might recite the Jesus prayer, which is the simple yet heartfelt repetition of the words, "Jesus Christ, Son of God, have mercy on me, a sinner," or, in simplified version, just the name of Jesus or "It is the Lord" (John 21:7). In Sufism, this remembrance is termed *zikr* and involves a repetition of the Islamic prayer "La ilaha illa 'llah" (Arabic: "There is no God but God"). The recitation of "the supreme name" *azam* is enjoined "with humility and in secret" and also "through fear and through desire"

(Qur'an 7:55–56). And again, "Verily in the remembrance of God that hearts find rest" (Qur'an 13:28).

In the Jewish scriptures, "The desire of our soul is to Thy name and the remembrance of Thee" (Isa. 25:8). The renowned German mystic Jacob Boehme extolled the untold power of invoking God's name when he said, "In the sweet name of Jesus Christ the whole process is contained." Indeed, this process of inner remembrance of the Beloved becomes the very life-breath of the lover. Tulsi Das, the highly regarded Bhakti poet of the sixteenth-century and author of the Hindi *Ramayana,* considered the repetition of Ram's name the sine qua non of all spiritual practice. He praises not only the glory of the outer name, but also simultaneously the splendor of the true name of God within. Tulsi Das writes:

Of the servant who repeats the Name of Ram with love.
How can the unsurpassable wonders then be told.[12]

In a similar passage in the Bhagavad Gita, the most holy scripture of the Hindus, Lord Krishna declares to Arjuna: "If you devote your mind to me, I promise you will become absorbed in me." The Hindu, like the Christian or Sufi, by invoking the name of God, abandons his or her own existence for that of the Lord. The lover who has invoked the holy of holies experiences the divine form itself, as his or her heart opens and closes like the lotus before the sun of existence. By this invocation, the lover invites the divine presence to enlighten every fiber of his or her being.

The Buddhist, when invoking the divine name of the Buddha Amitabha, "enters into the golden halo of mercy" and finds security in the blessed Light that Buddha called "the sonorous sound." As Frithjof Schuon has made clear:

Amida is Light and Life; His name carries the faithful towards the Western Paradise (Sukhavagt), the faithful allows the solar name through to its consummation, to the west—he follows it right "into the beyond" leaving the world behind him in the night—he follows this sun which having traversed the "round of existence" is thus gone (tathagata) or which is gone, gone not to return, gone to the other shore's gate (paragate, parasamgate).[13]

Meeting a Spiritual Guide

The previous short survey has listed some of the ways in which different cultures use the name of God in prayer and meditation to remind them of their spiritual discipline. In many religious traditions, the first step the seeker must take, after undergoing the necessary preliminary preparation, is to choose a guide or spiritual friend. As we have indicated, it may take a lifetime of preparation to enter into a relationship with such a being.

Accepting a spiritual guide into one's life is a profound decision, and the meditation at the end of this chapter is, in part, a way of testing the ground before embarking upon such a relationship. The choice of guide is a momentous decision, not to be entered into lightly. The wrong choice could have long-lasting adverse effects upon the soul. If a soul is sincere, however, it will be guided to a competent spiritual master at some point in its journey.

The following meditation will help to clarify and bring into focus the "archetypal Beloved" that is right for you. In Jungian terms, this would imply bringing forth from the collective unconscious the image of perfection and beauty that most resonates with your own inner propensities, background, and capacities as a human being. In a mythological context, we are envisioning the supreme hero, saint, or Divine Beloved, the being who, as Joseph Campbell suggested, has the power to transform and transfigure everyday pathos into mythos. This exercise is designed to be a means of attunement to the great sea of potentiality within which we all live and breathe.

There is a powerful story about the response of a destitute prostitute as she encounters her Beloved for the first time. Here is how she describes Him:

His mouth was like the heart of a pomegranate, and the shadows in his eyes were deep. And He was gentle, like a man mindful of his own strength. In my dreams I beheld the kings of the earth standing in awe in His presence. I would speak of His face but how shall I? It was like night without darkness and like day without the noise of day. It was a sad face and it was a joyous face. And well I remember how once He raised His hand toward the sky and His parted fingers were like the branches of an elm. And I remember Him pacing the evening. He was not walking. He Himself was road, above road, even a cloud above the earth that would descend to refresh the earth. But when I stood before Him and spoke to Him, He was a man and His face was powerful to behold. And He said to me, "What would you, Miriam?" I did not answer Him but my wings enfolded my secret, and I was made warm. Because I could bear His light no more, I turned and walked away, but not in shame. I was only shy, and I would be alone, with His fingers upon the strings of my heart.[14]

Allow this image to stay awhile in your heart and thoughts. Then, as the image fades, picture the master in this story facing you. Capture the emotional intensity of the meeting and make it your own.

Meditation: Meeting a Spiritual Guide

Choose a quiet spot, either alone or in the company of spiritual friends, after you have put to rest the "everydayness" of the world. You should restrain your senses and remain aloof from emotional upheavals for a period of time. If possible, create a prolonged period of "sacred space" in which you can turn within to meet your Beloved. For the American Indians, all nature was sacred; their temple was the sky overhead and the earth below. In whatever form best works for you, create a simple, quiet, holy ground for this exercise.

After making yourself quite comfortable, bring your mind to focus on the image of the Beloved. It does not matter whether you have met your Beloved before; all you need is to long for the personification of this One in whatever form he or she may take.

Allow your whole body to relax completely. Feel the preoccupations of the day floating gently away from you as you are enfolded in your own sacred space.

Allow your mind to fade to gray, and provide the mental space for your own divine friend to appear. Begin the process by visualizing the activities of the friend as he or she might go through daily life. As the friend walks, imagine his or her gestures. Does the friend float across the earth; does he or she glide, or just stroll?

As you imagine this being, bring to focus how the friend interacts with people. Does he or she bow, raise the hands in prayer, or simply shake your hand? Does this being smile as you approach?

Now imagine this being opening up to you. What does the friend say to you as you meet? What exact words does he or she use? Listen closely. How, exactly, does your friend speak? Are his or her words gentle or firm? Are they soft, musical, compassionate, or simply sweet and humble?

Imagine your first glance at the friend's face. What questions arise in your mind? What doubts? What thoughts cross your mind as he or she talks and looks at you? Do you speak? What goes on inside you? Examine yourself closely.

Examine your friend closely; focus intently upon him or her. What arises in your heart of hearts as you open up to your friend? Are you longing for him or her? Are you apathetic, joyous, or nervous? Examine your feelings, your responses. Examine your doubts. Be totally honest about your feelings.

While you hold those thoughts in your mind, gently awake from the meditation. Know that this meditation was more real than any act or meeting you have ever known.

Know that you have met your Beloved, if only for a moment, and that meeting, which was outside of time, must one day enter time. The Beloved is the very life of our life and the more we awake, the more we move in our friend's being.

Following Page:

Rama Shoots Arrow at Radha
Metropolitan Museum of Art, New York

In this detail from a lively Hindu drawing, Rama aims his bow at Radha, attempting to wound her with the joys of love, while Krishna is summoned (not shown). The arrow that pierces the lover is unique in that it never goes deep enough to slay his or her individuality. Instead, it remains embedded in the lover's heart, never allowing the lover to forget the Beloved. Both Radha and Krishna are in essence one, and this intrinsic identification is eventually realized by the lover. Sur Das speaks on behalf of Radha: "You become Radha and I will become Madhava, truly Madhava (Krishna). This is the reversal which I shall produce."

Chapter Four

The Valley of Sincerity: The Vale of Tears

O Restless heart, come, let us weep,
let us toss in pain,
Why think now of sleep?
We have a night that has no dawn.

—Darshan Singh[1]

The return to the primordial state of at-one-ment and gnosis is a return through a valley of the most intense pain. This process could well be called, in Keats' phrase, the "vale of tears." These tears represent, both literally and symbolically, the purifying process at work. At the very simplest level of meaning, tears represent the recognition by the soul of its separate and fragmented existence.

The lover is deep into the primordial quest for the essential rebirth or rediscovery of the animating and revivifying process of what Carl Jung called "self-individuation." Something must die in this process in order for the new spirit to unfold, purified and pristine. That something is the attachment to sensory pleasures, impure desires, and meaningless and prideful pursuits.

This stage is the *apatheia* (purification) of the early Christian fathers and the practice of *pratyahara* (restraint of the senses) of the Yoga Sutras. During this stage, the lover is required to withdraw his or her sense organs and develop contentment and internal concentration.

Tears are a wonderful symbol of this aspect of the journey, for such tears arise from the molten depths of the lover's yearning and pathos. As the lover polishes the mirror of his or her heart, powerful currents of love begin to surge in his or her veins, burning to ashes everything except the object of love. This internal burning in time becomes the very inner essence of the lover's condition.

During this station, four fascinating developments occur, which mark successive degrees of purification. First is the recognition of the Beloved's beauty. Second comes profuse burning tears. The third is characterized by intense regret and agitation. And lastly, the thought and longing for the Beloved seizes the mind of the lover.

In many respects, this stage is simply the first act of the long and bittersweet play of separation that is to follow. But few lovers at this point have even the slightest hint of the agony awaiting them. The beauty of the Beloved has so captured their hearts and so bewitched their senses that the path ahead remains veiled and concealed. For a lover, intoxicated by endless streams of love, light, and beauty, which appear to emanate effortlessly from the Beloved, no such long view is possible. The eyes of the lover see the Beloved as the very fountainhead of beauty in the world. And indeed the Beloved is, for the lover has fallen into the trap and is now helplessly caught. This recognition is the first of these phases. One gnostic tells his own story:

> *Everything is illuminated by the Beauty of Thy face alone,*
> *Every "man of heart" is desirous of Thee only,*
> *O Bestower of unique beauty, who bestoweth it on the deserving,*
> *All are really lovers of Thy Beauty only.*[2]

The inner vision of the Divine Beloved is not, however, vouchsafed to the lover until his or her appreciation for the grandeur of the Beloved reaches an apex of longing. Such yearning cannot be attained until the lover forgoes all other pleasures for the vision of the Beloved. Life has no meaning unless it be embedded in the context of the Beloved's love. The cry of the helpless lover at this stage is:

> *Would that I would forget all pleasures save the pleasure of Thy*
> *love.*
> *And the pang of thy love shall replace my life in me.*[3]

The Vale of Tears

The second phase of this station, which spontaneously follows the first, is the vale of tears. During this phase, the lover nearly drowns in a sea of tears, which appear to gush from an inexhaustible well within his or her being. In conjunction with this, there appears an agitation and restlessness that is relieved only by the physical presence of the Beloved or by an act of pure revelation from within. All outer pleasure becomes insipid and meaningless. The lover cries for the transcendent rapture of the Divine Beloved, and nothing else will satisfy his or her longing.

During this phase, there may be "yelling, howling, and lamentation, because love has not yet taken over the whole of the lover's being." But as Ahmad Ghazzali (Al-Ghazzali's brother) notes, "Once the affair reaches perfection, and love conquers the lover's domain of being, then these things are withheld, and lamentation is replaced by observation [of the Beloved's form], and leanness [of the lover's existence], because impurity has been replaced by purity." Ahmad Ghazzali describes the process in these words:

> *In the beginning when I was a novice in love,*
> *My neighbor could not sleep at night from my whimpers.*
> *But now that my pain has increased, my whimpering has decreased.*
> *When fire takes over something completely, smoke dwindles.*[4]

The Christian saint John of Ruysbroeck, in his masterpiece *Spiritual Espousals*, describes in great detail the unique and baffling state in which the lover finds himself or herself after some period in this station:

The lover, after receiving the call to unity with the inner Christ, and after tasting this transport of love, experiences an interior restlessness which will scarcely practice or heed the dictates of reason, unless it obtains what it loves. This interior transport consumes a person's heart and drinks his blood. The heat which is here felt from within is the most intense of a person's entire life. His corporeal nature is secretly wounded and consumed without being acted upon from outside, and the fruit of the virtues ripens more quickly than in all the modes which have previously been described.[5]

In this state of inner restlessness and oblivion, the lover may experience intense sorrow or the sweetest joy. Neither experience lasts long, however, and both often appear inwardly as one. One unknown poet wrote that it was "as if the entire body were being consumed from within by an interior fire and the yearning of the heart pours out the eyes like the sap from burning wood." These torrents of tears are often uncontrollable, and yet the true lover has not an ounce of self-pity but is rather propelled by the tears to make greater and greater sacrifices for the Beloved.

In the ancient Vedic scriptures, one of the Gujarti hymns cautions those who think they might avoid the inevitable "crucible of fire":

The pathway of love is the ordeal of fire.
The shrinkers turn away from it.
Those who take the plunge into the fire attain eternal bliss.
Those who stand far off looking on
are scorched by the flame.
Love is a priceless thing only to be won at the cost of death.
Those who live to die, these attain,
For they have shed all thoughts of self.[6]

In the mystic literature of the East, pearls are often used as a symbol for tears. These tears are pearls of great importance, for they contain all the secrets of love itself. The anguish of separation produces tears, which initiate a welling up of the soul into a state of supreme concentration. This crystallization of concentration within the soul is an act of perfect prayer, for it reconnects the soul with the Divine Beloved. In this sense, the psychology of purification is the act of perfecting prayer or dialogue with God. The profusion of tears that any true lover sheds paves the way for ultimate union with the Beloved. One poet has remarked:

I did not weep until my heart was lost.
So strange the bartering of love appeared.
I gave the shining jewel of my soul,
To buy these pearls my tears.

Rabia Basra, a celebrated Muslim saint, was once asked whether her prayers started first and then God came, or if God came and she then started to cry. She replied, "The moment tears burst out of my eyes I realize that the rain-laden clouds have come; I start my prayers and I find God there."

Tears, then, are a gift of grace from the Divine Beloved because they are the flowers that precede the fruit of union. Although Buddhism does not correlate its meditative states with stations of love, it does correlate them to states of concentration, called *jhanas* in Theravada Buddhism. Not surprisingly, these states of concentration are in many respects just different aspects of the experience of love. For the states of love cannot be accessed without intense concentration. What has been termed "access meditation" (*upacāra-samādhi*) is the first of the eight jhanas. In this preliminary station, the seeker overcomes what are known as the five hindrances: sensual desire, ill will, sloth and torpor, restlessness and agitation, and uncertainty and doubt. At this stage, however, the seeker's concentration is in an unstable state. He or she may enter states of deep concentration but cannot hold that concentration (jhana) for very long.

Similarly, the lover's gross sensual desires are overcome and he or she is not bothered by anger, worry, sloth, or depression. The endless oscillations of the mind have not come to a complete halt, however. In this state of deep yearning, the heart effortlessly inclines to God. Here the lover has torn asunder the gross veils of worldly dross and waits expectantly for the Beloved to appear. Though the lover has left the dusty streets of sensual desire, his or her inner mind is still active on much more subtle levels, unperceived by the conscious mind. The subconscious mind must be fully cleared; and this journey is never fully known by the lover. The lover's mind has been brought to a state of relative stillness, however, and experiences a wholly new perception of reality. The conscious mind achieves a new singleness of purpose and purity of intent. At the same time, the unconscious mind has come closer to the eye of inspection and the knife of a discerning intellect.

Inner Restlessness

The fruit of this phase ripening in the heart of the lover is an *inner restlessness*. Once the lover has experienced the state of inner bliss, the soul is restless to return to it once again. Each new encounter with the Divine Beloved produces a greater sense of agitation. Sant Kirpal Singh remarked that when this remembrance of the divine becomes overpowering, "there is no sleep for the eyes, no rest for the joints, for such a person can have no peace unless he sees his Beloved."[7]

Another poet observed: "Oh, mathematicians, you have calculated how long is the day, the night, the year; how long is the night for the anguished heart which cries for its Beloved?" The seeker experiencing this state cries out:

Without seeing the Beloved, sleep does not come;
This separation has now become unbearable.[8]

Often, while passing through this state, a seeker is advised by well-intentioned friends to cease the searching and desiring for God that is causing such discomfort. But the seeker has no choice, for his or her heart has been enraptured for all time. Guru Amar Das, the fourth guru of the Sikhs, when passing through this state, rebuked his friends:

Do not utter such words,
for even in this pain, there is sweetness.

This burning restlessness is part of the process through which every true seeker passes to some degree. Kabir was well aware of the necessity for weeping and inner restlessness:

Whosoever got Him, did so with tears;
could He be had with laughter and joy,
none would be without Him.[9]

The Persian Sufi mystics made a distinction between two types of tears: "Tears which develop through love for the Beloved, which are shed for your Beloved are called *ann-soo;* they are real tears. Tears caused by disappointment, unhappiness, or disillusion with worldly mundane affairs are called *een-soo;* the latter are not tears in the true sense of the word."[10] It is only the tears shed in love and soulful longing for God that are considered true tears in the world of mysticism.

If we study the lives of saints, we will find in many of them a period when they wept profusely while experiencing the pain of separation. The Prophet Mohammed would humbly say: "0 Allah, bless us with a weeping eye." In the Hindu tales of Krishna, the God-intoxicated lovers shed many a tear in divine longing for Krishna.

Tears, then, represent a perfect conclusion to, and about-face from, the previous period of *intimacy.* The lover, who at first coveted the priceless blessing of the master's personal affection, now treasures his or her own burning tears. It is not that the personal attention of the master is unappreciated when it is experienced, but the lover's primary nutriment now comes from the molten waves of love from his or her own inner treasure of love.

Regret

The results of this process develop into the third phase of *sincerity*, which some Sufis call *regret*. The word "regret" usually implies a lost opportunity. But in the present context, "regret" means a deepening of the feelings of separation and a fear of being deprived of the inner blessings of the Beloved. The poet saint Hafiz in describing this state remarks:

> *O thou jewel of a beloved!*
> *I plead before thee my woe of loneliness!*
> *Without Thee I feel the nearness of death,*
> *the hour demands that thou come to me.*[11]

This phase of intense regret has several specific aspects to it. The twelfth-century Sufi saint Al-Ghazzali gives us a vivid description of some of the more pronounced characteristics of this phase.

First, he says, the lover does not lament any loss in the world besides that of the remembrance of the Lord. And if, for a moment, he or she forgets the Lord, the lover prays to the Lord to be forgiven that transgression. Quoting Hazrat Abu Bakar, Al-Ghazzali notes, "He, who has tasted of the Divine Love, is stopped from desiring anything in the world or seeking the company of any individual."

A second aspect of this regret is the sleeplessness that gradually overtakes the lover. Al-Ghazzali notes, "He who claims to love Me, and yet sleeps at night lost to himself and his surroundings, he is false in his profession of love for Me, and has not felt separation, for he seeks not Me, but his own self-indulgence, and that is not the way of lovers."[12]

Seized by the Thought of the Beloved

This phase of deep regret inevitably leads to a state of near continuous remembrance, in which the mind is completely and *continuously seized by the thought of the Beloved*. When the inner mind has become sufficiently purified through the constant repetition of the Beloved's name, or some attribute of the Beloved, the inner radiant or light form of the master makes its appearance.

The link between continuous remembrance of the Beloved and the appearance of the light form of the master must be clearly understood by the lover, for it is a subtle key that unlocks the doors to the mansions of the Beloved: By bringing the image of the Beloved to mind, the lover sets up a powerful thought-form connecting himself or herself to the Beloved.

These thought-forms, or "elementals," as the Christian gnostic and healer Daskolos explained, possess a life of their own. They create from the ethereal energy of the universe a wholly new psychic and spiritual reality for the lover. As this remembrance is literally etched upon the physical and subtle mind through constant repetition, it becomes part and parcel of the lover's noetic or causal body. Whatever becomes imprinted at the causal level must in fact be manifested as a physical and gross reality. This process is only possible, however, when it is accompanied by an intense aspiration arising from the heart of the lover. Thought alone is insufficient. Only a heart that is agonized in longing can create such entirely new realities.

At this point, the thought of the Beloved literally seizes the lover, wherever and whatever he or she is doing. The lover has aligned his or her entire existence to coordinate with the Beloved's. The two beings, though perhaps separated by thousands of miles, remain in constant telepathic communication so long as the lover is engaged in remembrance. When this state becomes effortless, the lover passes through the corridor of sincerity without any knowledge of self or his or her own striving.

The lover who has arrived through the corridor of sincerity has been thoroughly tested on the grindstone of tribulation. He or she has moved unfailingly through deep despair and endless weeping to agitation and mercurial restlessness, which appears to be without end. Intense regret has produced sleeplessness and constant repetition of the Beloved's name. Cleansed of ephemeral desires and self-indulgence, the lover, steadied, now plunges headlong into the ocean of remembrance of the Beloved. Finally, the lover offers himself or herself to the crucible of fire and tastes the depth of real separation.

Chapter Five
The Valley of Separation:
The Fire of Burning

This secret has revealed itself to me;
Love is not a dew drop;
it is a spark of fire.
—Darshan Singh[1]

In the fourth stage of the journey, sometimes called the fire of separation, four movements occur that mark phases in the evolution of the process of separation.

First, the heart of the lover experiences an acute sense of inner burning that consumes all save the thought of the Beloved. In the second phase, the constant invocation of the Beloved's name produces an intense and perfect concentration in the living moment. In the third phase, ironically the trials and tortures of love are transmuted into the cure for separation. In this phase, everything, including the harshest of suffering, is viewed as a special boon from the Beloved. In the last phase, the lover moves from willing resignation to a conscious surrender of all aspects of his or her life. In the last phase, since the door of union is not open and the lover cannot take nutriment directly from the Beloved, oppression becomes the lover's most valued sustenance. Here oppression does not imply physical torture, but rather the indifference and humiliation experienced at the hands of the Beloved.

Inner Burning

The symbol of love at this stage is fire, for the lover not only is burning, but has also become nothing but a flame of yearning. Some ancient authorities refer metaphorically to the face of the lover being inflamed with the image of the Beloved. For the lover, good and evil have ceased to exist. Farid-uddin Attar, author of *The Conference of the Birds*, describes this phase appropriately:

> *In this valley love is represented by fire and reason by smoke.*
> *When love comes, reason disappears.*
> *Reason cannot live with the folly of love.*
> *Love has nothing to do with human reason.*[2]

One who has been tested in the fire of love begins to realize the necessity of separation, for the very process of separation brings the lover into the embrace of the Beloved. For the lover, the moments in which he or she is acutely aware of individuality, and hence separation, are excruciating. In the Christian scriptures, this fire of longing is beautifully expressed in the Song of Songs, a book filled with passionate and ecstatic images consistent with the lover's feelings of intense separation. In this fire that consumes the lover's being, she cries out (Song of Songs 3:1–2):

> *Upon my bed by night*
> *I sought him whom my soul loves;*
> *I sought him, but found him not;*
> *I called him but he gave no answer,*
> *I will rise now and go about the city,*
> *In the streets and in the squares;*
> *I will seek him whom my soul loves.*

Such periods of heartbreak, as Rabbi Nachman expressed it, are the very essence, in Judaism, of turning one's face to God. He described these periods of intense inner yearning as "screaming to God." The great Hasidic master was also quick to point out that there is a world of difference between "heartbreak" and "depression."[3] In the former state, one is in a state of self-forgetfulness and spiritual yearning; in the latter, one is consumed in the quicksand of self-delusion and despair. The difference here is critical for the lover to understand, for the former implies the abandonment of self and the world, while the latter enmeshes one further in the delusion and constantly shifting mirror of self-infatuation.

When the lover reaches this phase of intense inner aspiration, every second becomes agonizing, for there is no peace without a glimpse of the Beloved. In this state, the lover calls out with heart-rending cries, pleading for help and grace. In this state, even one moment without such remembrance of the Beloved is like a death for the lover. Such intense longing produces a perfect cleansing of the mind's mirror. A certain poet remarks:

No sleep for the eyes or peace in the body,
for he comes not nor writes.
O friend, if I do not see my Beloved,
Then how can I live through this dark night.[4]

With the passage of time, this phase culminates in a profound reorientation of the lover's faculties of perception and understanding. In the course of this mysterious inner alchemy, the lover realizes, in the words of Sant Kirpal Singh, that "what you see is you." In such a state, the lover who wants to see himself or herself will see only the image (*pakyar*) of the Beloved. A poet aptly describes this visionary experience:

I have your image in my eye so much,
that whatever I perceive, I think it is you.[5]

In such a condition, every atom appears endowed with the image of the Beloved. The greater the yearning, the greater will be the experience of this state. Such states of bittersweet separation are in fact orchestrated by the Beloved Himself. Hazur Baba Sawan Singh, a saint of the twentieth century, maintains that "whom He [the Master] loves the most is always sent away for a while." Only in this way can the pangs of separation reach the pitch of yearning necessary to still the continuous oscillations of the mind. The lover at first complains of his lot but in time realizes that this gift only accelerates the union with the Beloved.

For the true lover, time itself is an enemy, for it deludes one into thinking that life is endless. Time is a deception of those enmeshed in the pursuit of the world. The lover knows the value of each moment, however, and cherishes it as a continuous gift from the courtyard of union. Every moment is an opportunity to remember the Beloved. And every moment spent in forgetfulness of God is like a miniature death, for time cannot be reversed. In this sense, every moment utilized for its highest purpose is immortalized, for it achieves the perfection of its potential.

A story about Kabir relates how he forgot the name of God twice. As a result of this loss, he wept inconsolably the whole night. Toward dawn, Lord Ram Himself came down to comfort Kabir and to assure him that He was well pleased with His disciple's unflagging love and practice. Kabir, still uncomforted, replied, "I have missed two opportunities to say the name of Ram. Never can I regain the joy of those lost names."[6] It is not difficult to find similar passages in other scriptures. Guru Arjan writes in the Guru Granth, about his own experience of separation:

> To cease His remembrance, even for a second,
> All happiness leaves and misery results.
> My mind is desiring Thy Darshan [company]:
> Like the rainbird in anguish,
> The thirst remains unquenched—there is no peace,
> I am living like that without the Beloved's Darshan.[7]

Merging in the Moment

For the lover experiencing these pangs of separation, all apprehension about the future or the past drops away like autumn leaves in the wind. So intense is the concentration in the present that it produces a merging in the moment. One becomes, as the great Rumi once said, "The son of the moment."

It is this coming into the present that the ordeal of separation produces. And paradoxically, it is precisely here—in the present moment—that eternity is found. For the experience of separation appears infinite to the lover. He or she becomes lost in its timelessness. There is no escaping it. In this timelessness, the lover finds not only the face of his or her Beloved, but the face of eternity as well. As the Zen Master Seppo said:

> If you want to know what eternity means, it is no further than this moment. If you fail to catch it in this present moment, you will not get it, however many times you are reborn in hundreds of thousands of years.[8]

The Cure for Separation

When separation itself seems endless, and the awareness of the lover becomes centered in the present moment, it becomes its own cure. At its zenith, the process of separation produces, to the lover's surprise, a state of intense inner bliss. This bliss is a further deepening of the process of self-abandonment. Since there is nothing left for the lover to take nutriment from, and union is still not possible, the lover finds himself or herself at the table of love and feasts upon his or her own pain. A poet by the name of Hawa describes this condition graphically:

> *None enjoy such luxury as I enjoy in Thy love: My companion is*
> *pain,*
> *My wine is blood, my rissole is the heart, my hors-d'ocure is woe.*[9]

This state, though difficult to recognize because of its paradoxical nature, has been referred to in various religious scriptures. In the Christian scriptures, Saint Paul refers to being made perfect in his weakness. The cosmic and deeply personal significance of his suffering is made clear to him when he quotes the words of Jesus Christ (the only time he does so in all his voluminous writings): "My grace is sufficient for you, for my power is made perfect in weakness" (2 Cor. 12:09 ESV). In this state, Paul cries out, "For the sake of Christ, then, I am content with weaknesses, insults, hardships, persecutions, and calamities. For when I am weak, then I am strong" (2 Cor. 12:10 ESV).

Although Paul may not explicitly state that pain is desirable, he nevertheless implies that torment is an ingredient in gaining his perfection. If there is a difference here, it is simply in the mode of resignation and not in kind. The poet Hawa not only accepts his anguish, but also actually derives pleasures from it. He has surrendered to the process completely and exhibits no sign of personal preference. In Saint Paul's case, pain and anguish are only different aspects of an endless flow of blessings experienced as he surrenders to the Divine Beloved. The language may be different, but the theology and results are quite similar. Sarmad, the great Jewish mystic, portrays this paradox most artfully:

> *The universe*
> *is a kaleidoscope:*
> *Now hopelessness, now hope*
> *Now spring, now fall.*
> *Forget its ups and downs:*
> *Do not vex yourself:*
> *The remedy for pain*
> *is the pain itself.*[10]

Constant Invocation

Such a condition gradually evolves into a continual prayer, which is unlike prayer as we normally describe it. This continual or incessant prayer involves no ordinary associations with the world and is actually embedded in the deepest humility. The Sufis have called this phase *hawa* (intense supplication), but, in reality, it is more than simply "asking." It is also affirming the divine identity and the cosmic embrace of the Beloved.

The effectiveness of this supplication depends directly upon the sincerity and humility in which it is offered. If it contains even the slightest association with the world, it is flung back into the face of the lover. The lover has to be, as Saint Ignatius Loyola has said, "a true renouncer, renouncing all other thoughts except that which he loves."

In due course, the lover realizes that it is clearly not a matter in which he or she has any say. Rather than turn away from the Beloved (as some unfortunately do), however, the lover surrenders the whole affair into the Beloved's hands. This act of surrender produces a profound sense of endurance and resignation.

The lover soon realizes that any yearning that does not touch the deepest level of the heart is prey to the tyranny of time. The path of love demands constancy and unlimited patience on the part of the lover. It is here that many a lover rolls in the seas of doubt and despair.

The reason for the flight of the Beloved is that union with Him is not an insignificant matter. Using the female gender for the Beloved, Ahmad Ghazzali explains that "just as the lover must submit himself [to the Beloved] so that he is no longer himself, the Beloved must also consent to his being Her lover. So long as She has not consumed him entirely from inside and taken him as part of Herself, and so long as She has not received him completely, She escapes from him."[11]

When, however, the lover has been completely tamed by love, then he or she no longer wills even his or her own union with the Beloved. Shah Latiff, a Hindu mystic of the fifteenth century, gives us some inkling of this endurance in the following lines:

True lovers love and adorn themselves
with the scaffold as garments,
And consider it a matter of shame
to hesitate and lag behind.
They accept by troth,
wagering their life for it.
A hundred times a day they rush to climb it [the gallows].
Bidding good-bye to comforts,
they suffer cheerfully to woo love.[12]

Mira Bai, a saint of the sixteenth century, expressed this theme with similar pathos:

Kahn [Her Master] *I bought.*
The price he asked I gave.
Some cry, "Tis great" and others jeer, "tis small."
I gave in full, weighted to the utmost grain,
My love, my life, my soul, my all.[13]

The embrace of this endurance is so profound that every so-called obstacle appears to be another gift from the Beloved. The lover, as Meister Eckhart once said, includes all occurrences in his or her being, seeing them all as part of God's being.

For the lover experiencing this truth, whatever he or she pushes aside is exactly that part of himself or herself that must come under the eye of scrutiny. Carl Jung talks about how humans often thrust away the dark side of their nature, refusing to acknowledge or explore it. This is precisely the area, however, that can teach us the most.

For the lover experiencing this truth, whatever is happening, both the seeming light and the seeming dark, is God's gift. Whatever the lover excludes is that aspect of God that he or she has not integrated within. It is at this critical moment that the will of the Beloved and the will of the lover begin to merge.

Total Resignation

In the last phase of this passage through the fire of separation, called resignation, the lover consumes both union and separation. The lover realizes that both union and separation have, in essence, nothing to do with love. Love is beyond the constraints of time, space, and all phenomenal appearances. It is in this context that the lover begins to taste the delicate feast that is the gift of his or her surrender. Surrender is not some sort of passive defeat. On the contrary, surrender represents the soul's dynamic and co-creative role in the will of God. The lover now has a new place in the scheme of creation. He or she realizes both his infinite insignificance and infinite worth at one and the same time.

Many Western readers equate the word "surrender" with giving in. But to the mystic, "surrender" means giving up the limited will in order to participate in the infinite will. It is a highly conscious and supremely empowering act in which God embraces the lover as a conscious co-worker in the divine plan. The immensity of this act releases powerful currents of love into creation. The lover is at last, by providing God with a heart capable of holding His awesome creativity and power, augmenting the force of the life impulse sustaining the entire creation.

It is a curious fact that, whether one is following the eightfold path of Buddha, the path of nondualism of Shankara or Ramana Maharshi, or the path of love of Kabir, all paths begin to resemble one another at this point. For in essence, all paths lead to a state of intense surrender to the supreme will of the Creator. Once the lover resigns everything to the hands of the Beloved, the question of choice is no longer a possibility. Choice exists only when the illusion of separateness and therefore individuality prevails. As soon as the reality of the Beloved's grandeur is known, the question of individual action separate from the divine is impossible.

Seen from this vantage point, the greatest "sin" is our separate will. Our existence as separate ego is a denial of the sublimity of Love. "I-ness" presupposes the possibility of individual action. But when the lover transcends his or her ego, there remains no other door for the lover to open, no other direction in which to look but into the face of the Beloved. Shah Latiff expresses this theme with great clarity when he says, "every fiber of the lover is turned into a veritable string of the guitar, which repeats His name every moment. He never complains or utters a sigh." Only when the flute is completely empty can the sweet music pass through it. Saint Paul refers to this state cryptically when he says, "For to me to live is Christ, and to die is gain" (Phil. 1:21 ESV).

To touch and heal those places in the heart of the lover that as yet have not been touched by love requires the magical touch of the Divine Beloved, for it is the Beloved alone who knows exactly where those areas are and how best to heal them. Lovers who understand this secret submit joyfully to the rebukes and trials that the Beloved places in their path. They have become empty of the business of self. Hafiz, the great poet and mystic, beautifully captures the essence of this state of surrender:

> O Lover! Separation and Union are none of your business.
> Seek only to resign yourself to the Will of the Beloved.[14]

In the Christian tradition, as long as the individual characteristics of the lover remain, union with the Christ power is not possible. Crucifixion, in this sense, is the death of the outer characteristics of the lover and the resurrection of the Beloved in their stead.

Chapter Six

The Valley of Concealment: Expansion of the Heart

*The blood of my desires
Has been shed a thousand times,
But no one has ever found
a tear drop in my eye.*

—Darshan Singh[1]

The fifth station of love has been termed by certain Sufis "concealment," and by Christians "unceasing prayer." It may also in some respects resemble the Buddhist stage of recognizing the unwholesome nature of sense objects and all mental phenomena accompanied by quick and flawless perception. This stage is marked by four distinct aspects, according to the Sufi tradition.

First is distancing of the Beloved from the lover. This estrangement increases as love elevates in perfection. With it appears the spontaneous and implicit outer obedience to the commands of the Beloved without thought, consideration, or choice. Second is the expansion of the heart, in which all creation is embraced as a manifestation of the Beloved. In the third phase, the lover experiences a new kind of love that shows a wanton disregard for the conventions of society and the prison house of conditioned and habituated thinking. To be sure, the lover has not penetrated beyond intellectual perception but sees clearly its gross inadequacies and the utter meaningless of societal norms. This, from the point of view of the world, is often construed as a kind of reckless madness. Fourth is the concealment of love and the veiling of the secrets of love from all but the Beloved.

Distancing from the Beloved

In the first phase of this valley of concealment, the lover continues the ascending process of resignation already established in the last phase. Here the lover continues to estrange himself or herself from his or her own intellect. The lover seeks to continually subjugate his or her reason and will entirely to the will of the Beloved. Having come to see through intense self-analysis the falsity of his or her own belief systems, the lover learns to withhold intellectual and personal judgment. The very thought of disobedience here is a departure from the court of love. To understand this, one must realize that reason itself cannot enter the abode of love. Baba Farid, a Sufi from the Indian subcontinent, tells us:

> *Love here is fire; its thick smoke clouds the head,*
> *When love has come the intellect has fled.*[2]

Farid tells us that reason or understanding dispels the fire of love. Love burns in the fire of longing and not from reason or intellectual disputation. Baba Sawan Singh went so far as to say that "we should throw hundreds of books into the fire if necessary, for our hearts should be a garden of the flowers of love."[3]

At this crossroads of love, outer knowledge stands in contradiction to the truths of love. Reason is a faculty of the mind and not an aspect of the essence of love. Whoever is not prepared to renounce speculative reasoning will never enter the abode of love. Meher Baba, the Indian master, would often caution his disciples that "no amount of intellect can take us to God. No amount of austerity can enable us to attain God. It is only when we love Him and lose ourselves in Him that we attain to unity. It is only by the feat of love that we lose ourselves, that the two become one."

The lover who would proceed further must abandon the baggage of "perception" and discursive reasoning. Unquestioning obedience to the Beloved is not attainable unless intellectual judgment is withheld. The judging mind is the last stronghold of the intellect. But God cannot be fathomed, nor can His ways be intellectually understood. Submission to the will of the Beloved is submission to the slavery and dominance of love. How can the hand of freedom ever touch the skirt of the lover? Such "freedom" would imply the loss of the Beloved.

Expansion of the Heart

When we abandon the attempt to use our minds to apprehend God, we see the world for the first time without the distorting spectacles of thought. Suddenly, the world seems vastly more immediate and powerful than the lover ever imagined. Saint John of the Cross tells us:

> At times a man wonders if he is being charmed and he goes about with wonderment over what he sees and hears. Everything seems so very strange even though he is the same person as always. The reason is he is being made a stranger to his usual knowledge and experience of things.[4]

The process of becoming a stranger to the known and the Beloved rearranges the lover's perception of the world. Attar uses metaphor to describe the immensity of this spiritual change that occurs:

> *He will perceive the marrow, not the skin —*
> *The Self will disappear; then, from within*
> *The heart of all he sees, there will ascend*
> *The longed-for face of the Friend.*
> *A thousand secrets will be known*
> *When that unveiled, surpassing face is shown.*[5]

Here Attar is speaking of a love that discovers the infinite power of its own self-sufficiency, while simultaneously realizing that this creative power is reduced to powder in the presence of the supreme love. The word here is "expansion" because, as Attar so graphically explains, all normal phenomena become insignificant in the face of the Beloved. The entire emotional body and outer personality begin to dissolve as the lover goes through a deep metamorphosis.

At this station, the lover's ideas of the Beloved also undergo a radical shift. The lover realizes that the outer Beloved has, in reality, nothing to do with the essence of love. The physical form is merely the steed of the Beloved. It is not its commander. The real form of the Beloved is love, and light, or, as it is referred to in the New Testament, "the Light of the World."

In the mature state of love, the lover will see no "otherness" in the being of the Beloved. The Beloved is the perfect manifestation of God's plenty, the perfect vehicle for the transmission of God's will. The nameless absolute dwells in the "Word made flesh." Jesus said, "For I have not spoken on my own authority, but the Father who sent me has himself given me a commandment—what to say and what to speak" (John 12:49).

The Madness of Love

There is a wonderful story that illustrates the dilemma of the intellect unable to submit to the will of the Beloved.

Lord Krishna remarked that he had a pain in His stomach, the cure of which could only be effected by the heart of a living person. He told one of His closest devotees to get such a heart from somewhere; otherwise He would die. The devotee was so concerned that he ran at once and began searching from house to house, but no one was willing to cut out his or her heart and give it.

All day he searched, until finally at night, exhausted and desperate, he came to the home of a prostitute. When he told her of his mission, she said, "All right, here, take it," and thereupon cut out her heart and handed it to him. The devotee ran with the heart to

Lord Krishna and sank at His feet. Lord Krishna said, "Oh, you finally found one person who loved me enough to give her heart! But what about yourself? Are you not supposed to be my closest devotee? Are you not a human with a heart as well?"

When we speak "mad love," we imply a state that transcends the dualities of life and death. For the lover, mad with love for the Beloved, nothing is impossible, and nothing inevitable. The will of the Beloved is the very life of the lover.

There is a remarkably similar story from the history of the Sikhs that illustrates the ease with which a true lover offers himself or herself in the service of the Beloved. It so happened that on one occasion the master, seeking to test the faith and obedience of the disciples, asked for a volunteer on whose body he could test one of his rifles. At his request, not one but two disciples jumped forth, vying to be the first to test the rifle. The youngest stepped forth and pleaded with the guru that the others had already tasted the gift of surrender to the Beloved, but he was young and should now be given this opportunity.

The second and elder Sikh pleaded that the younger one would have many more times to offer his life in the service of the master but that he was old and should be permitted to die in honor. The guru, knowing the inner condition of both, fired two shots from his rifle. One bullet hit the younger, and the other hit the older of the two. In that instant, neither was hurt, but both were spiritually transformed and the glow of illumination shone from their faces.

These stories, which may appear fanciful at first reading, illustrate the love that can obey with reckless disregard for world and self. "Which of you," the New Testament asks, "by taking thought can add one cubit to his stature" (Matt. 6:27 KJV). When reasoning and understanding have been displaced by the transcendent and supremely harmonizing force of love, the heart expands, realizing its own connectedness to everything it perceives. Reason is one of the most opaque veils separating us from the face of the Beloved.

Absolute Secrecy

In the last phase of this corridor of estrangement, the lover is required to maintain absolute secrecy with regard to the condition of his or her heart. Love is a secret, not only because it arises from the pretemporal domain, but also because words mar the sublimity of its perfection. One mystic wrote, "Love is covered and no one has ever seen it revealed. How long will these lovers boast in vain?"[6]

The lover, then, despite all agonies, reveals nothing of his or her love to the world. It is a state that cannot be described, as love, like God, is only fully revealed in the pretemporal grandeur of love. In the realm of temporality, love must be concealed, for its very nature cannot be fully experienced in the realm of time. How, then, can it possibly be explained or understood via words?

Those who speak the language of love speak it without words. The problem here, as Sant Darshan Singh has explained, is that the lover can neither explain his or her inner condition nor keep it entirely from the view of others. The path of love is as fine as a razor's edge:

> So the outward display of one's intoxication, one's love for the Master, may uncover a certain pride. It may lead to the expression, however subtle, of the ego, although it is hiding behind the veil of one's enthusiasm. In any outward show of one's bliss, elation, or ecstasy, it is essential to make sure that there is not the least semblance of pride. Otherwise, the intoxication will wither away in no time.[7]

In contradiction to the Western model, where it is quite in order for the lover to display his or her love, mystic love "in the East is always a silent yearning, a silent pining, and nobody is supposed to know about it."[8] One of Sant Darshan's verses captures this thought eloquently:

I have borne all atrocities, all eccentricities, all
idiosyncrasies, all sorts of torture and
indifference, for the sake of my Beloved;
Yet I have never complained.[9]

Even the very stars and flowers are to be kept from the secrets of love. The bird of love does not alight upon the tarnished flowers of the world but within the heart of one whose love is like an invisible cool breeze in the midst of the heat of the world. According to the principles of love, even tears are a blemish, for tears are an expression of love that has already lost its dignity.

In yet another verse, Sant Darshan explains the loss of honor that a lover undergoes when his or her tears become a "visible display of love":

The moment the molten heart can be seen
in the form of a tear,
our love no longer remains a secret;
it loses its sublimity.[10]

This betrayal of the eyes is a great loss of honor for the lover, because love is a secret and must remain a secret. For Westerners, this concept of secrecy may at first seem strange, for why indeed should one conceal such a wonderful state of love?

There are several reasons for this concealment. In the first place, as mentioned, there can be no adequate description of the lover's relationship to the Beloved. To attempt to describe it is to demean it. Its sublimity is its beauty. By speaking, the lover asserts his or her own individuality. Any assertion on the part of the lover is considered a sign of spiritual immaturity and a sacrilege. One cannot assert one's own love, only the love of the Beloved.

Yet the difficulty of this stage is that it is also not possible to hide completely the secret of one's love within oneself. A gnostic explains this unique predicament when he says:

However much I may conceal the pang of my love for thee,
My foolish tears betray me.
My pale face betokens my inability to bear separation from thee.
It throws into open the secret hidden in me.[11]

Jesus cautioned his followers on a number of occasions against flaunting their good works. "Good works" refers both to giving alms and to loving God. Here secrecy does not mean refraining from works of charity but concealing the love of God from the jealous eyes of the world—giving but making sure "that your giving may be in secret. And your Father who sees in secret will reward you" (Matt. 6:4 ESV).

The lover who completes this phase of concealment moves forward with the jewel of the Beloved hidden within the deepest recesses of his or her heart. Unable to express anything of his or her love, the lover walks the path of self-abandonment and humility.

Chapter Seven

The Valley of Estrangement: The Three Faces of Renunciation

*O men of lust, beware of entering
this land of love.
Here you will find only
the cross and the gallows.*
—Darshan Singh[1]

t is said that once a princess named Zaibul-Nisa went to Sarmad, a Jewish saint of the seventeenth century, and requested of him the rare boon of God's love. Sarmad replied:

*O friends, the burning passion for the Lord
is not granted to the avaricious,
nor the moth's love for the flame
to flies that hover 'round filth.
It takes ages to get the revelation of the Lord.
This wealth is not doled out to all and sundry.*[2]

The path to inner purification, as Sarmad pointed out, is not lined with roses. For the lover, the struggle for inner unification is a path of great sacrifice and trial. All passions must gradually be subdued and in their stead one sole passion remains: love for the Beloved. It is not, then, simply sexual love that must be mastered, but anything at all that may come between the lover and the Beloved. Sensual love is but one aspect of the Hydra-headed face of desire. For the lover, three distinct aspects emerge in the perfection of love.

The Sufis have referred to these as the three faces of blame. These "faces" are turned, one toward the world of creation, one toward the lover, and one toward the Beloved. They represent the gradual and sometimes sudden severing of the lover from himself, the world, and even the Beloved. Ahmad Ghazzali explains that the:

> face toward the world of creation is the sword of the Beloved's jealousy; it consists in keeping the lover from paying attention to anything other than the Beloved. The face toward the lover is the sword of time's jealousy and it consists in keeping the lover from paying attention to himself or herself. Finally, the face toward the Beloved is the sword of love's jealousy; it consists in making the lover take nourishment from nothing but love, and in compelling him or her to seek nothing from outside [love's essence].[3]

These three "faces" are the means by which the lover severs himself or herself from all things other than love, even if it be the Beloved, for even the Beloved may function as something "other." As we can readily see, the lover during this phase, and indeed throughout the journey, is engaged in a continual process of assertion and negation: assertion, in that he or she asserts only the existence and reality of love; and negation, in that he or she negates all aspects of "otherness" within.

When Sant Darshan Singh invites lovers to the cross and the gallows, this is part of the process of negation. Desire is the movement of the soul away from the Beloved, for in the perfect state nothing is allowed in the sanctuary of love except love itself. The poet has summed up this perfection of love:

> *I would be disloyal*
> *and could not claim to be in love with you.*
> *If I ever cried for your help,*
> *You may impose union or separation,*

I am untouched by these two,
your love is enough for me.[4]

Blame toward Oneself

The first face of blame requires the lover to transcend the influence of the five outer senses, which are reflected in the major vices: lust, greed, attachment/avarice, and jealousy. In this phase, the physical plane is transcended and the elixir of the Beloved's glances within replaces attachment to outer enjoyments. The lover may still not be free from subtle reflections of these attachments on the inner planes, for that is not fully accomplished until much later stages. The veil within has been drawn aside, however, and the lover begins to subsist on the inner radiant form of the Beloved. The centering of the lover's attention in the radiant form of the master reflects not only the ability to absent himself or herself from creation, but also the ability of at-one-ment with the essence of Love.

Blame toward the World

During the second phase of blame or renunciation, the lover is called upon to utterly deny himself or herself. In this process, the five inner senses and their attachments to inner phenomena are transcended. Here the ego finds nowhere to hide and comes against the full force of love. Here the lover acknowledges the essential illusory nature of his or her ego, the source of all "I-ness," evidenced by pride, egotism, vanity, and the drive to accomplish. All acts that are motivated by the narrow, self-centered ego tarnish the pristine face of love. Here even the thinnest hair of self-deception becomes a wave that washes one off the path. The sublimity of love demands the lover renounce even renunciation out of love. We have ample testimony to this thought in both Hindu and Judaic-Christian traditions. In *The Imitation of Christ*, Thomas à Kempis writes, "If thou wilt be my disciple, deny thyself utterly."[5] And in the language of the great nondualist Ramana Maharshi, "Renunciation is non-identification of the self with the non Self."[6]

The paradoxical nature of renunciation is revealed succinctly in the Tao Te Ching (XXII):

He who has little will receive
He who has much will be embarrassed.

To understand this process, it may be helpful to perceive the lover as gradually divesting himself or herself of all the shackles of "phenomena" first, and then of "nomena." Even the finest sheath of subtle astral and mental matter must be removed, for such matter covers the true reality of love. This peeling away of the self reverses the process of perception. The divesting of mind (*manas*), intellect, (*buddhi*), perception and memory (*chitti*), and, in the later stages, ego (*ahankar;* the root cause of individuality) proceeds in direct proportion to interiorization of love.

Blame toward the Beloved

The last phase of this journey through "estrangement" is reflected in the third face of blame, which is directed toward the Beloved. It is at this phase that even the Beloved may act as something "other" and become an obstacle to the lover's realization of the ultimate essence of Love. So long as the Beloved is perceived as other than love, as other than oneself, as other than Supreme God, the reality of union is not possible.

There is a story in the Mahabarata that aptly describes this sense of otherness with regard to the Beloved. It is said that once Krishna went on a tour to Benares, about one hundred miles from Brindavan. Although Udho pleaded with Krishna to take him along with him, He instructed Udho to remain behind. For nearly two weeks, Udho was languishing in a state of separation, shedding copious tears all the while. Krishna neither appeared in his meditations nor returned from his tour. Finally, after nearly two weeks,

Krishna appeared to him. Udho asked despairingly why had it taken so long for Him to appear.

Krishna replied, "Had you thought I was the life of your life and the breath of your breath, I would have appeared instantly, but since you thought I resided in Benares, it took me two weeks to get here by the road."

The Beloved is not simply a form that appears within, but the supreme center of the universe, the supreme center of our own existence. At this stage, the lover realizes there are no limitations to the infiniteness of the Beloved. It was to this reality that the Persian mystic Shabistari alluded when he said:

In all things,
See but One,
say but One,
know but one.[7]

Or in the words of the contemporary saint Ananda Moyi Ma: "The inward and the outward are indissolubly united and form a single great eternal current."[8]

Or in the words of Hermes:

Not that the one is Two,
But that these two are one.
The One is neither I nor Thou, this nor that.

Rumi personified that quest for love in every fiber of his being. For Rumi, the Beloved is not found or sought or even "become," but is that essence in which we drown without our own awareness. In fact, the world itself is not other than love; it is merely the veil of forgetfulness, which instantly dissolves when the Beloved is recognized. Rumi writes:

Seek him in the placeless, he will sign you to a place.
When you seek him in the place,
*   he will flee to the placeless.*

As the arrow speeds from the bow,
 like the bird of your imagination.
Know that the Absolute
 will certainly flee from the imaginary.[9]

Rumi says emphatically that there is no place where the Beloved is not. One cannot seek Him anywhere, for thought itself flees from the Beloved. The realm of desire will always flee from the realm of illumination, and illumination from that of desire. So, too, does the Beloved flee from every aspect of "otherness," which is only the shadow of the real. The real is not and cannot be sought by an act of will, imagination, or thought, but is who we are when illusion is removed. It is this realization that is the essence of unity.

Sri Aurobindo gives us some indication of the experience of the lover as he approaches with his purified heart the threshold of love's chamber of unity. Here knowing is experienced as an expansion of the heart and the closing down of the outer senses:

> One begins to know things by a different kind of experience, more direct, not depending on the external mind and senses. It is not that the possibility of error disappears, for that cannot be so long as mind of any kind is one's instrument for transcribing knowledge, but there is a new, vast, and deep way of experiencing, seeing, knowing, contacting things; and the confines of knowledge can be rolled back to an almost unmeasurable degree.[10]

The words of the great Sufi Master Farid Attar give us a poetic description of final estrangement of the lover from the world of shadows and the kaleidoscope of empty forms:

> In this state of the soul a cold wind blows, so violent that in a moment it devastates an immense space; the seven oceans are no more than a pool, the seven planets a mere spark, the seven heavens a corpse, the seven hells broken ice. Then an astonishing thing, beyond reason, an ant has the strength of a hundred elephants, and a hundred caravans perish while a rook is filling his crop.[11]

Following Page:

Rosette Bearing the Name and Titles of Emperor Shah Jahan
Metropolitan Museum of Art, New York

The mandala, in both Sufi and Hindu iconography, is a reflection of both the cosmos and the cosmic process. The following example is a Mughal work (ca. 1645). It represents all things moving in perfect symmetry from the Absolute Unity through its theophany back to Unity. To the mystic encamped in the palace of Unity, the mandala reflects the surrender of the self and the reintegration of the many into the One. Here the mystic becomes a being of true insight and, holding up the cup of divinity, sees all things as if through a glass clearly.

Chapter Eight

The Valley of Unity: The One in the All and All in One

He is hidden in every instrument,
in every song and melody.
All creation reflects His glory.
There exists not a sparkling wave nor a fiery star
that does not owe its radiance to His Light.

—Darshan Singh[1]

The words of Sant Darshan above are the echo that resounds at the door of unity. Anyone who passes through that door speaks with the same tongue. Part becomes whole, or as Farid Attar more perfectly remarks, "There will be neither part nor whole; the Being I speak of does not exist separately; everyone is this Being, existence and non-existence. Everything is perishing except His Face, unless thou art in His Face [essence] do not seek to exist. Whoever is uttering 'I' and 'we' at the door, he is turned back from the door."[2]

When the lover sees none but the Friend, and Him alone, then, as Abd al-Qadir Jilani, the great Sufi of Baghdad, says, "We see none but our Friend, Him alone we desire, and go after no one else. We have passed by ourselves and cut asunder all other ties."[3] In Christian terms, this move toward the universal unity has been described as the entering of the Son into the infinite Being, so that even Sonship is subject to the absoluteness of God. In First Corinthians (15:28), it is explained, "When all things are subjected to him, then the Son himself will also be subjected to him who put all things in subjection under him, that God may be all in all."

In a similar vein, we hear from a Jewish mystic who paints a picture of unity that echoes the ecstatic Hindu devotional ideal of an all-consuming and embracing presence. The lover bears, in reality, no label and if he has a label, it is the face of His Beloved:

O Lord of the universe
I will sing thee a sound.
Where can't thee be found?
And where can't Thou not be found?
Where I pass — there art Thou.
Thou, Thou and only Thou.
Thou are, Thou hast been and Thou wilt be.
Thou didst reign, Thou reignest, and Thou wilt reign.
Thine is Heaven, Thine is Earth,
Thou fillest high regions,
And Thou fillest low regions.
Wheresoever I turn Thou, Oh, Thou art there.[4]

The Encampment of Unity

The recognition of this unity is the quintessence of all revealed spiritual traditions. To the lover, the realization of unity comes in degrees as he or she advances through the corridors of the divine unity. Each step a deeper dive into the ocean of infinite love. The first step is the recognition of the Beloved in all, in which the Divine Beloved becomes the repository of all existence, including the lover's. Krishna tells Arjuna on the battlefield of this state, "Whoever sees me in all, and all creation in me, he is my Beloved. The clay is the same, formed into different shapes by the Potter; all the same, they are clay with conscious entity residing therein."

The second step toward the consciousness of unity is the recognition of the self-sameness of that Beloved to oneself. No longer is the Beloved other than oneself. In the Hindu scripture the Chandogya Upanishad Brahamana, it is said, "That which is the finest essence—this whole world has that as its Self. That is Reality. That is atman [Supreme Self]. That art thou, Svetaketu."[5] The Lankavatara Sutra reaffirms this reality: "Self Realization is based on identity and oneness."[6] Self-realization is based on identity and, to enter into it, the disciple must be free from all presuppositions and attachments to things.

Cessation of Desire

One of the most memorable extracts from the Buddhist text the Dhammapada is the Buddha's Victory Song. It describes the dismantling of the superstructure of illusion and ego. Buddha describes each lifetime as a house built by God. These houses or lifetimes are made necessary by the soul's desires. Of the cessation of such desire, Buddha says:

> *Seeking the builder of the house,*
> *I have run my course in the vortex*
> *Of countless births, never escaping*
> *the hobble of death:*
> *Ill is repeated birth after birth.*
> *Householder, thou art seen!*
> *Never again shalt thou build me a house.*
> *All of thy rigging is broken,*
> *The peak of the roof is shattered;*
> *Its aggregations passed away,*
> *Mind has reached the destruction of cravings.*[7]

Desire ceases when we realize our own divine perfection, own Buddha nature. We realize that we ourselves are the Beloved we have been seeking. Distinctions fade away. When the ego dies, there is only love, neither Beloved nor lover, both of which are aspects of a conditioned existence. It is desire or craving that creates conditions, and their removal shatters illusory existence. The Mundaka Upanishad (Ch. 2, ii) affirms, "The luminous Brahman dwells in the cave of the heart and is known to move there. It is the great support of all; for in It is centered everything that moves, breaths and blinks."

Unity expresses itself in concrete form in the outer world as action that exhibits no personal interest or motivation for selfish ends. When we read of the selfless acts of the great saints and masters, we often wonder how anyone can act with such total personal disregard. Yet the vision of the unity precludes any other type of action. The love that has transcended its own self-interest cannot fail to express a unitive and life-affirming ethos. Here, it is not what one does that is important, but the quality of love that is manifest in those actions. The experience of selfless love, which began as a gift from the Beloved, is now channeled back to all creation.

There is an exquisite story that encapsulates this unitive vision in action. During the Mughal reign, many battles were waged against one small band of Sikhs who resisted subjugation. During one of those battles, it was noticed that Bhai Kaneya, who was in charge of giving water to the wounded, was giving water not only to the wounded Sikhs, but also to the Muslims who had fallen in battle. The other Sikhs accused him of high treason.

After much debate, the case was brought before Guru Arjan Dev, the spiritual leader of the Sikh faith at the time, and a spiritual master as well. It was explained to him that Bhai Kaneya was hindering the Sikhs from winning the war for their religious freedom by reviving the enemy's wounded at the very moment when they needed water the most. Arjan Dev heard the accusations in a quiet and pensive mood, knowing all the while the real state of his disciple. Then he asked Bhai Kaneya to respond to the allegations against him.

Bhai Kaneya, in his usual gentle manner, said, "Sir, I give water neither to the Muslims nor to the Sikhs, I give water to you and you alone. Wherever I see your effluent light I pay my obeisance. Wherever I see your radiant face I give water to you."

The guru replied, "This is the only man who has truly understood my teachings. And from now on Bhai Kaneya will not only give water to the Sikhs and Muslims, but he will balm and bandage them as well."

Perfection of Outer Conduct

During this stage, as the story of Bhai Kaneya illustrates so well, the lover perfects his or her conduct in the world. The true lover now views everything as an aspect of the essence of love and therefore makes no distinction between enemy and friend, good and bad, right and wrong. When the awakened soul pierces beyond the veil to the noetic and unitive vision, he or she witnesses all forms embedded in one reality.

Every atom of the universe pulsates in the divine essence of love. The true lover harmonizes with every being because he or she experiences them as himself or herself. His or her experience is always inclusive of others, never exclusive. True compassion, like that of Bhai Kaneya, arises because there is no room for distinction or diversion.

Ramakrishna Paramhansa, in trying to describe this state, once said that "it was like seeing every form wrapped in a silken cloth of light. The forms themselves were there but they were of a dream-like quality. Each form, whether an ant or an elephant, was the Supreme Reality."

The direct result of this state is the transformation of the outer personality and the perfection of virtues. The lover swims in the ocean of equanimity and compassion while serving others selflessly. The lover who experiences this realization becomes a person of true insight. Things do not happen to him or her but in him or her. The divisions between inner and outer disappear. Whatever is happening is happening in and through the cosmic body. In this state, the lover eats through the mouths of others, sees through the eyes of others, and feels through the heart of others. Service to others is found to be service to the one Beloved. What else can the lover do now except serve the light that he or she is?

Mother Teresa of Calcutta was once asked, "Mother, how does it happen you are able to do so much, and why are you in this state of joy?"

"My dear," she said, "it is because I am so deeply in love."

"But, Mother, you're a nun."

"Precisely," she said. "I am married to Jesus."

"Yes, I understand, you're married to Jesus. All nuns are."

"No, you don't understand," she countered. "I really am so in a state of love that I see the face of my Beloved in the face of the dying man in the streets of Calcutta. I see my Beloved in the day-old child who's left outside our convent and in the leper whose flesh is decaying; and I can't do enough for my Beloved! That is why I try to do something beautiful for God."[8]

All in One and One in All

This sacred vision of the All in One and the One in All, which Mother Teresa so beautifully describes, is an act of supreme self-surrender. The vision is not static but dynamic, and compels the lover to act as any lover would in the service of his or her Beloved. Wherever the lover sees the Beloved, he or she is called to action. The lover is committed to the service of all humanity, for that very service is an act of love to the Beloved. This outward action of the lover is not something that occurs only at one stage; it occurs from the very beginning of the search for the Beloved. But what is unique to this particular stage is its grounding in ecstatic vision. Here vision is with the "inner eye" of spirit and not the "eye of flesh and bones." This eye is that through which lovers see creation and it is an all-encompassing and embracing vision of unity.

When serving the Beloved, in whatever form that service may take, the lover no longer notices any difference between the Beloved and his or her own most interior self. So who is serving whom? For his or her actions to be described as "service" is astonishing to the lover, for there is no recollection except of love. The great Zen masters have tried, in their unique way, to explain this mystery. The poet-monk Sengtsan alludes to this:

In the World of Reality there is no self,
There is no other-than-self.[9]

It is this mystery that nourishes the lover's continuous bewilderment, for concepts are meaningless in a state of love. When the lover is charged with this self-effacing love, the power of love is present in a sacred, ever-deepening, ever-widening sphere of love. Everyone the lover meets is empowered and connected to that same cosmic fire of love that consumes everything except the Beloved.

It is not accidental that this chapter appears at this point in the lover's evolution toward total unity. The lover is entering into the causal or noetic plane of the universe, in which the basic building blocks of the universe are revealed. Here the outer qualities of the lover begin to disappear. If he or she was a contemplative, he or she no longer remains one; if he or she was a lover, he or she is now without a Beloved. Whatever quality he or she had is now lost to him or her. Attar says of this state that the lover "has been reduced to nothing in Thee."[10]

This transcendence of relative values and ethics is indeed a difficult task, for it involves the dismantling of the subtlest aspects of personality. The primary quality that supports personality in illusion is ego. And therefore whatever we most pride ourselves in is shattered. This is not ordinary suffering, but transpersonal, for we are not speaking about the outer garments of personality as it is seen by others, but the very fabric of consciousness itself, which is interwoven with ego. Here the entire storehouse of karmic effects, going back countless ages, is rent asunder, and the knot between the conscious life force (*shakti*) and the unconscious (*prakriti*) is untied for good. It is as if the mirror in which perception itself is perceived is shattered. A lively Hindu folk song to Kali, the symbol of the destroyer, epitomizes this stage:

> *Confoundress with Thy Flashing sword,*
> *Thoughtlessly Thou has put to death*
> *my virtue and my sin alike.*[11]

Like rags and tatters that have tripped the lover up and hidden his or her true nature, the lover now sheds the last scraps of separate existence. It is existence itself that is rooted out, to be replaced with pure being, which is beyond cause and effect.

The process of Creation or, as it is known in Persian mysticism, the arc of descent, ends with total entanglement in what one is not. The arc of ascent is about to close where the lover now returns to the original point, the origin of Origins, love itself. Every idol is broken, every illusion shattered, and the last stitches of the thread of ego begin to unravel. Finally, the robes of pure being, which is pure and perfect love, are draped upon the soul. As the Sufi poet and mystic Hatef Isfahani exclaims:

> *There is one and only One;*
> *There is no God but HE.*[12]

Following Page:

Mohammed's Night Journey
Metropolitan Museum of Art, New York

The Night Journey of Mohammed represented in this illuminated manuscript culminates in his reaching the seventh heaven (top of the causal plane). Here, enveloped in a golden cloud, he bows before the Throne of Allah in an ecstasy approaching annihilation. The Almighty communicates to him ninety-nine ineffable words of the Law and commandments.

Chapter Nine
The Valley of Ecstasy: Beyond Acceptance and Rejection

What does it matter if we never regain
our senses?
This day O Cupbearer, pour forth as much
as we can drink.

—Darshan Singh[1]

f the lover is fortunate enough to reach this station, he or she becomes a true citizen of the land of love. Having rent asunder the veils of intellect and reason, the lover quaffs the cup of ecstasy and comes to the fountainhead of the primal source of creation. During this most marvelous station, four movements are articulated as the lover journeys forth.

First, the Beloved reveals to the world the inner condition of the lover's heart. The coveted secret of love between the Beloved and the lover becomes an open book for all to see. In the second phase, the lover escapes the confining prison of self-awareness and passes beyond all sense and sensibility in the ordinary context. Here the lover enters into the sea of self-oblivion and tastes the infinite bliss of his or her nirvanic Self. In the third phase, the lover transcends all intellectual discernment, rejection, or acceptance. This world has lost all meaning and the only joy is in the vision and service of the Beloved. In the fourth phase, the lover plunges into the sea of intoxication, never to see the shores of his or her existence again.

In the final phase of ecstasy, the lover has no self that is other than the Beloved. Immersed in a sea of rapturous love, there is not the least concern whether he or she is accepted or rejected, whether he or she is in union or separation. In this beguiling condition, when the lover meets the Beloved, he or she will "disappear" in direct proportion to the maturity of his or her love. The lover has become, as a human individual, completely transparent.

Immersed in the rapturous inner light and music, Kabir explains the wonder of the thunderous sound of the sacred inner music as it resounds throughout all creation:

> *Think of it, knower of Brahma.*
> *It's pouring, pouring, the thunder's roaring,*
> *But not one rain drop falls.*[2]

Revealing the Lover's Heart

In the first phase, which the Sufis have called *ishtar*, the Beloved gives full publicity to the inner condition of the lover's heart. The lover, however, has become so immersed in the ecstasy of love that he or she cares for neither the respect nor the disapproval of the world. The Beloved, however, in seeking to test the purity and steadfastness of the lover's condition, sets a clever trap. The trap consists in revealing to others the perfection of the lover's inner attainment. The lover, left to his or her own, would not dare to reveal this secret love before the multitudes. The lover's desire is to remain concealed from the world, which would in the end only create distraction.

At this point, many difficulties may arise that cause great agitation, turmoil, and anguish. The lover may find the bait of the world's attention too much to bear, and succumb to worldly adulation and praise. Yet, if the lover remains steadfast, he or she remains unaffected by the adulation and praise of others, instead diving still deeper into the ecstasy of his or her own heart.

There is, in fact, a whole tradition in Christian hagiography that documents the lovers of God as fools of Christ, who commit extravagant acts in an attempt to hide themselves from the eyes of the world. There is a similar tradition in Islam among those known as *malamatiyah* (people of blame), who strive to hide from the world through self-conscious acts of blame. In India, too, there has always been a tradition of the fierce or mad *must* who may at times violently abuse people in order to preserve his or her privacy. The mystic poet Hafiz seems to have had this in mind in composing this *ghazal*:

> *O fill my cup with wine, with seasoned wine, with wine of bitter taste,*
> *But with the strength and force to fling the strong on solid ground.*
> *Oh let me drink that wine which has the gift*
> *To save my thoughts, if for a while,*
> *From tear and wear of worldly care.*
>
> *The world exalts the base, denies the lordly soul repose.*
> *For from the palate of the sense wash off, O heart,*
> *The taste for greed or cov'tous deed.*
> *Go far away from lips of eager hope,*
> *From tongue of longing deep,*
> *Their sweet or bitter deep,*
> *O Haste, bring us wine*
> *And drown in wine the sham insulting lures of boors.*[3]

During this phase, the lover's love crystallizes into something sublime and permanent. No longer fearful of outward distractions, the praise or blame of the world, the lover now moves inward, united with, and in remembrance of, the Beloved. Here the inner vision of the lover is opened and the secrets of eternity can be read like an open book.

It is here that reason is truly sunk as it is immersed in a sea of "pure witnessing." Kabir, with his characteristic simplicity, put it this way:

Nectar in a bundle,
took it down from my head.
When I tell them it's one
They say two-four instead.[4]

Oblivion

In the second phase of this process of ecstasy, the lover not only loses all sense and sensibility in an ordinary context, but also becomes oblivious to his or her own condition and ultimately even to his or her own ecstasy.

During this process the lover is neither an ascetic nor a *sadhu*, neither of this world nor of the next world. The lover is aware solely of not being aware. The consciousness of the lover is almost destroyed in the process of witnessing the Beloved's beauty. Yet the lover retains just enough individuality to taste of the bliss of this wondrous state. The lover becomes reckless to attain the final consummation of union, and now "charges forth like one drunk and finds his or her way to the *Kharabat*, or tavern of love." Matilda of Magdeburg, an early Christian saint, spoke knowingly of this wine and of its potent charms that render the lover "poor and naked":

Wouldst thou come with me to the wine cellar?
That will cost thee much:
Even thou a thousand marks
It were all spent in one hour.
If thou wouldst drink the unmingled wine
Thou must ever spend more than thou hast,
And the Host will never fill thy glass to the brim.
Thou wilt become poor and naked,
Despised of all who would rather see themselves in the dust
Than squander their all in the wine cellar.[5]

As Matilda colorfully states, this divine inebriation leaves the lover stripped of all that he or she took to be himself or herself. What remains is the majesty of ecstasy. In a more analytical vein, the mystics tell us that the physical body is composed of five elements: earth, water, fire, air, and ether. The subtle body consists of seventeen elements: five organs of perception (eyes, nose, ears, mouth, and skin); five of action: (sight, hearing, smell, taste, and touch); the five vital airs; and *manas* (mind) and the bliss covering. All except the bliss covering (*anandamai kosha*) have been peeled back, as it were, from the self-luminous consciousness that is love. What remains is the bliss covering, which is none other than the self-consciousness of one's own bliss. This bliss is a reflection of the infinite bliss of the perfect nature of love. It is the reflection of love viewed in the mirror of the lover's mind.

Acceptance and Rejection

If the Beloved favors the lover and he or she endures this favor without losing sight of the Beloved, he or she gains the state described in the Qur'an: "His sight never swerved nor did it go wrong." In this state only the slightest thread of ego remains to prevent the lover from realizing his or her complete identity with love itself. It is at this point that the lover enters into what the Sufis have called the cave of union.[6] In this cave, the poor helpless lover goes mad with love for the Beloved. During this madness of love, the lover has not the slightest concern for whether he or she is accepted or rejected, whether he or she lives or dies. As one poet said:

> If a thousand lashes of "By no means canst thou see Me direct" are lashed upon the lover's back, even then the lover will go reiterating the cry: "Show thy Face to me that I may behold Thee." Even in the face of the totally impossible, the lover cries out, "It is possible."[7]

The Sea of Intoxication

This great ocean of bliss is the lover's true abode. In fact as Sant Rajinder Singh has said, it is "our destiny to swim in the divine intoxication." Under the spell of this wine, the entire reality of the lover is turned upside down. Saint Isaac of Syria, one of the early Christian fathers, seems to have spoken to this point:

> Love for God is naturally ardent and when it fills a man to overflowing, leads the soul to ecstasy. Therefore, the heart of a man who experiences it cannot bear it, but undergoes an extraordinary change according to its own quality and the quality of the love which fills him. He is as one out of his mind. A terrible death is for him a joy, and his mental contemplation of heavenly things is never broken.[8]

In this state of divine ecstasy, the lover's absorption is so profound that there is nothing that can divert his or her attention from the Beloved.

Al-Ghazzali reveals to what extent this madness takes hold of the lover:

> *Even if the gnostic were cast into the fire,*
> *he would not feel it, because of his absorption,*
> *and if the delights of paradise were spread out before him, he would*
> *not turn toward them,*
> *because of the perfection of the grace that is in him,*
> *and his perfect attainment,*
> *which is above all else that can be attained.*[9]

In this elevated state of primordial witnessing, the soul remains immersed in the rapturous strains of divine light and inner music. Here the brilliance and magnitude of this light is equal to 100,000 full moons rising. Such illumination extinguishes everything but the bliss of his or her own Light. Richard of Saint Victor, a little-known Christian mystic of the Middle Ages, hints at the predicament facing the lover:

For when the mind of man is carried beyond itself all the limits of human reasoning are overpassed.
For the whole system of human reasoning succumbs to that which the soul perceives of the divine light, when she is raised above herself and ravished in ecstasy.[10]

The great theologian and mystic Eckhart tells us of the state of ecstasy that is beyond rational communication. The experience of this love is far beyond all dualities of life:

If once a man in intellectual vision did really glimpse the bliss and joy therein, then all his sufferings all God intends that he should suffer, would be a trifle, a mere nothing to him; nay I say more, it would be pure joy and pleasure.[11]

In much of Eastern literature, and in particular Sufi poetry, the light that emanates from the *Murshid*, or guide, is referred to as the wine in the tavern of God. It is the God-man or Murshid who dispenses this wine, which proceeds directly from the "flagon" of the master's eyes to the various disciples, or "tipplers." It was this wine that Omar Khayyam immortalized in his *Rubaiyat*:

You know, my Friends, with what a brave Carouse,
I made a Second Marriage in my house;
Divorced old barren Reason from my Bed,
And took the Daughter of the Vine to spouse.[12]

The Spanish poet and mystic Nablusi, an early medieval saint, speaks of this divine intoxicant as well:

Wine signifies the drink of divine love, which results from contemplating the traces of His beautiful names [attributes]. For this love begets drunkenness and the complete forgetfulness of all that exists in the world.[13]

In such a state, there is nothing left but the Beloved.

Khawaja Hafiz spoke as one who would gladly forsake all for the Divine Friend:

None finds room in my heart save my Friend.
O Lord, give both the worlds to my adversaries,
My Friend is enough for me.[14]

Sant Darshan Singh uses remarkably similar language, though writing in the twentieth century in India:

Look at the overcast sky unburdening itself, O love,
Spill forth thy wine in a like measure, O love,
And let the wine of Oneness so overwhelm us, O love,
That all distinctions and divisions be lost, O love,
Thy divine vintage has at last cleansed me, O love,
Now unfold the mystery of the two worlds, O love.[15]

It is unfortunate that many Western readers are unaware of the subtle psychological and spiritual implications hidden in the verses of many Sufi, Christian, and Hindu mystics as well as those from other traditions. Their verses, as we have seen, are only adornment of a Sufi's dress; they do not even touch the "threshold of knowledge."

Ramakrishna, the God-intoxicated Bengali saint, went so far as to say even the tiniest drop of that wine of communion gives "ten million times more happiness" than any sensual enjoyment.[16] Still, with all this, the door of perfect love has not been opened. The test of this truth comes when the lover, in the act of seeing the physical form of the Beloved, "becomes agitated." This is because "his existence is provisionally borrowed and he faces non-existence. In the ecstasy of love (*wajd*) his existence is agitated, until he rests with the reality of love."[17]

As this love perfects itself, the lover looks so deep into the heart of love that he or she looks nowhere but within for the source of his or her nourishment. Marsilio Ficino, a Christian saint, indicates this state when he speaks about the highest degree of contemplation in which "it [the soul] becomes God, it becomes happiness itself."[18]

Thus, as the luminosity of love descends into the heart of the lover, the intellect (which is merely another covering of the soul) is discarded and true ecstasy manifests itself in direct proportion to its displacement. Sant Darshan Singh suggests to lovers the greatness of this love when he says:

Oh tell the darkness of intellect
To seek the madness of love,
For this madness is a beam of light,
And nothing but light.[19]

Fellowship with the Friend is unfortunately another dream of the imagination, because the lover can never become truly intimate with the Beloved. So long as the lover remains, the Beloved hides His face from the court of union. What we have become we can no longer experience as "other."[20]

Paradoxically, then, even ecstasy must be obliterated, because it is contingent upon or nourished by the state of separation. The lover, realizing that his or her condition of ecstasy is predicated upon separate existence, must decide between tasting the honey or becoming it. If the lover is fortunate, he or she plunges headlong into the sea of martyrdom and becomes the honey itself.

Some Eastern mystics refer to a final step in love in which the breath of the lover may acquire both the scent (jasmine) and the color of the Beloved, or the lover may even exchange physical forms with the Beloved. As the Beloved opens his heart in a gesture of final acceptance, the lover loses all awareness of even the slightest aspect of himself or herself. The illustrious Rumi sums up the plea of the lover for the wine of love and nothing but love:

Pour out wine till I become a wanderer from myself;
For in selfhood and existence I have felt only fatigue.[21]

Chapter Ten
The Valley of Bewilderment: Destruction of Ego

The flame has consumed the poor moth,
And it trembles at the thought of its own end.
—Darshan Singh[1]

uring this most baffling and perplexing station of the journey, the lover finds himself or herself in a field of paradoxes. This stage is also traditionally characterized by four phases. First comes the eradication of the heart or, to use Sufi language, *walah*, or *bewilderment*; second, the *destruction of ego*; third, the achievement of *flawless concentration*; and fourth, *perfect surrender*, of even the sense of surrender or, in Sufi terms, *fana fil-shaykh*, or *merger in the master*. All of these phases, however, interlock with one another and do not occur in a linear fashion. In fact, nothing about this journey is actually linear, for time itself is part of the illusion.

During the first phase of this journey, which masters have called bewilderment, the great paradox is that, although the lover has achieved to a great degree a unity in understanding, he or she, in a strange turn of events, forgets even himself or herself. If the lover is asked, as Attar says, "Are you or are you not? Have you or have you not the feeling of existence? Are you in the middle or on the border? Are you mortal or immortal? He will reply with certainty, 'I am in love but with whom I do not know. My heart is at the same time both full and empty.'"[2]

In this state the lover seems to lose all sense of control over his or her state and even the sense of existence is lost. Why does the lover lose the sense of his or her own reality and know nothing of his or her own condition? The reason is that the faculty of perception can no longer perceive itself. We "know" ourselves by the borrowed luminosity of our own minds. The mind, when it is perfectly clear, reflects the perfectly luminous radiant Self. When we remove this mirror, this knowing faculty, what is left is self-luminous love. It is unable to see itself through the witness of itself, but only through the Beloved. In Sufi terminology this is referred to as "losing one's heart," "eradication," or "astonishment."

Ahmad Ghazzali explains this paradox of union:

The lover attains Union only with being's disintegration,
self's disunion. The very union of his being,
the principle which holds his self together,
in his separation from the Union of love.[3]

"Losing the heart," of course, refers not to the physical but to the spiritual sense of one's entire reality. There is a beautiful Persian poem that points to this state of utter bafflement:

Why do you make a search for my heart,
for I do not know where it is.
Tell me yourself what is a heart.
I do not find its trace anywhere.[4]

Using the metaphor of the moth and the candle, Ahmad Ghazzali explains this precarious condition of the lover's lost being:

The moth has a means of travel—his powdery wings—
but the machine of flight is not the tool
by which he will attain to Union. His round of flight,
the "air of quest," extends no further than the

glowing sphere thrown by the candle into space.
Union with the flame is the station of burning;
Flight lasts no further than the fire's borders,
and once the moth surrenders his being to the lamp
he moves no more toward the flame, but feels
the flame now move in him. Fire's love
for the moth now penetrates his being.[5]

The lover's wings carried him as far as they could, but as he entered the fire, his wings were burned and he was consumed by the fire's light. The lover comes to know that the reality of union is attained through the gates of extinction. Union is not in the lover's hand. Though the lover in previous stages may have held out a "hope" for union, now he or she realizes powerlessness in the face of this all-consuming love. The lover surrenders everything and realizes the instrument of Union lies not with the lover but with the Beloved.

Kabir made it known just how difficult it is to go beyond our self-conscious ego:

So what if you dropped illusion?
You didn't drop your pride.
Pride has fooled the best sages,
Pride devours all.[6]

The state of love in which not even the tiniest particle of ego/pride is permitted is a profoundly rare state. In fact, it is a state that cannot be achieved by any act of will or individual effort, but only through the will of the Beloved. As Meher Baba reflects:

Divine love arises after the disappearance
of the individual mind
and free from the trammels of individual nature.[7]

Indeed, only a few hearts are fashioned for this extremity of love. Only a few hearts are ready to receive so complete a gift of love. Love, as one poet has suggested, is "that music which cannot be played on every instrument." The Indian poet Ghalib expressed this idea when he said, "Love is not controllable. It is a fire which neither can be kindled nor extinguished at will." To go beyond the ego, beyond the sense of "I," as Ramana Maharshi would say, is to achieve liberation.

Flawless Concentration

In order to achieve this state, however, the lover is required to perfect the art of concentration. Flawless and complete concentration, as Sant Kirpal Singh has noted, is only "another aspect of complete and total self-surrender. Whenever the 'self' enters the picture and the question of 'I-ness' arises, the single pointedness of concentration is dissipated and inner advancement is made impossible."[8] Wherever there is perfect concentration, "I-ness" cannot arise. The "I" of individuality no longer asserts itself, for it has been consumed in the image of the Beloved.

As the lover passes through this baffling state, he or she may experience ecstasy and grief, patience and impatience, yet understand not to whom they belong. In this most wonderful phase, love has penetrated into the innermost depths of the lover, and because of this, his or her external personality cannot comprehend the mystery hidden in the innermost center of his or her heart.

As love penetrates into the essence of the Beloved, it obliterates the self-conscious ego, which gives rise to the subjective cognitive understanding of reality. As it penetrates still deeper, the very heart of the lover is consumed by love. In this condition, the lover weeps in great grief, but, strangely, has no sense of for whom he or she is weeping. The condition is like that of a man who has fallen asleep and in a dream meets a woman who is without equal. They spend an entire day together. Upon awakening, he is unaware of where he has been or whom he has seen. He does not know whether it was a dream or a reality. Neither does he know why he is in tears.

In this story, the lover who fell asleep is the one who met his Beloved within, but upon returning, having lost his self-conscious memory, he cannot remember what happened. The lover is left in utter bafflement. The experience, however, is so profound that he cannot forget it either, for his heart was torn asunder. In this state, Attar said there is enough sorrow for "a hundred worlds."[9]

Perfect Surrender

During this perplexing state of affairs, the lover yields up the pearl of his or her heart and surrenders everything to the Beloved. The phase of surrender has been mentioned in almost all scriptures, and yet there are few who really comprehend the depth of its significance.

The surrender of the mind is the most difficult of all tasks; indeed, it is impossible without the grace of the Beloved. In the first place, one cannot surrender what one has no control over any more than one can give something that is not one's own. Why is this journey so impossibly difficult? Because it is impossible to attain what you already are. So perfect concentration is just another name for perfect love.

The paradox of this condition is that perfect concentration produces perfect witnessing and thus the lover no longer sees through the eyes of knowledge but through "borrowed eyes" of love. If we have assumed that love has penetrated to the innermost center of the lover, there is beingness without knowledge of it. The lover cannot perceive the Beloved except with the eyes of love. His or her "experience" of the Beloved is not through knowledge but through the absenting of himself or herself.

This state is like that of the man who was in love with a woman who lived across a mighty river. Every night he would jump into the river and swim to her. One night he exclaimed, when he saw a mole on her face, "Where did this mole come from?" She answered, "I have had this mole from birth. But for your own sake, do not go into the water tonight." He did not listen, went into the river, and died of cold.

This simple parable alludes to the fact that the love of the lover is a veil upon the Beloved, and the greater his or her love the less he or she sees of the Beloved. This example, in truth, is what is meant by self-surrender in its ultimate ontological sense. Kabir tells us also that once having surrendered everything—body, wealth, possessions, and intellect—we have to surrender the very "thought of surrender," or the seed mind.

Sant Kirpal Singh summarizes the qualities that make up the perfect state of surrender when he talks of "complete obedience born out of love, with no conditions, with no hope of any return, expecting absolutely nothing in return, with no choice left."[10]

In this state, there is no question of choice, for there is no reality other than that of the Beloved. Choice arises only when there is still some aspect of the interior heart that does not participate in love, or has not been fully subdued. Only a part of the heart that does not dwell fully in the Beloved can believe it has the choice of whether or not to be in the Beloved. Choice presupposes a sense of duality. In the exalted state of perfect self-surrender, even the sense of a separate existence has been consumed, and choice has no place. Meher Baba gives us some indication of the levels of self-surrender that the lover passes through to arrive at this stage:

- Those who do what the Master asks at all cost, but expect reward.

- Those who do what the Master asks, sacrificing everything and not expecting reward; but they do it because their surrender to the Master demands it of them.

- Those who have no thought of their surrender and are so completely resigned to the Master's will that the question of how, why, or when never enters their minds. These are the "fortunate slaves" that Hafiz advises us to become: "Befitting a fortunate slave, carry out very command of the Master without question of why or what."[11]

Love, in these ultimate states, does not descend into the blind alley of cognitive perception. Comprehension and apprehension are experiences viewed through the limitations of the faculties of sight, hearing, smell, taste, and touch. Ultimate spiritual realities, on the other hand, can never be known by anyone; they can only become. In this sense, we affirm what Saint Paul said when he remarked, "No one has ever seen God; the only God, who is at the Father's side, he has made him known" (John 1:18 ESV). To do so would be to assume that we can cognize God.

In Jewish mystical literature, the notion of self-surrender is a very old one and finds expression in many Kabbalistic texts. For the *zadik* (spiritual teacher), everything must be surrendered in the name of YHWH. In this primal act of surrender, the mystic tells us that "he who utterly surrenders his soul to the name of YHWH will dwell and establish its throne and glory."[12]

For the Jewish mystic, as with all other lovers, the act of "giving up the self" is central to the consummation of the lover-Beloved relationship. The point here is that no matter the religious tradition, the actual experience of union transcends the limited confines of both Eastern and Western theoretical dogmas. Mysticism, in fact, transcends all outer or exoteric aspects of religion, for religion conveys concepts about unity and not unity itself. C. G. Jung once insightfully observed that religions are, in fact, a defense against the religious experience.

Frequently, seekers, instead of trying to actually experience these transcendent states, choose to conceptualize them, and by so doing remove themselves one more step from the actual spiritual experience. Understanding is not being. It is a sign of a lover's spiritual maturity that he or she understands that he or she does not understand.

For the true lover who has awakened to the light of love, there is no seeing and no existence apart from the Beloved. In fact, there is nothing but the Beloved. The lover now, as Sant Rajinder Singh has said, "makes an offering of the ego at the altar of devotion to God."[13]

In proceeding through this valley, the lover passes beyond the confines of time and space. Here the lover is not tied down by the stations of *contraction* (spiritual sorrow) or *expansion* (ecstasy). Neither is he or she concerned with separation or union, delight or sorrow, or any changing state.

The lover, who was previously under the control of time, and hence subject to change, is now the commander of time and in the decision-making position. Having passed from all contrary states, the lover rests in the changeless state of God beyond time. In this realm, nothing can pierce the darkness of the black light save the all-luminous Beloved. And in order to pass through this realm, the Beloved absorbs the lover completely. The Sufis indicate this state by the phrase "becoming a hair in the Beloved's tress."[14]

Now having effaced the conditions of change and time, and completely shattered the idols of falsity, greed, and illusion (death, desire, and ego), the lover is ready to move to final union in the Beloved. The lover, having transcended the three bodies (physical, astral, and causal) and come to know the mystery of the origins of creation and the void of nothingness, is now empowered by the will of the Beloved to pass through the *Maha Sunn* of the Sant Mat saints, *nirodh* of the Buddhist Adepts, into a state of God beyond God or Par Brahm. This is the final journey of the perfected lovers and the final home of the soul.

Chapter Eleven
Unending Oneness: The Ocean of Infinite Love

I and the Father are one. —John 10:30

Who art Thou?
I am thyself.
—Jaiminiya Upanisad Brahmana III i.6

Everything is perishing except His face.
—Qur'an 28:88

ome Sufis have called the station of unending one-ness the valley of *destruction and deprivation;* others have referred to it as *enslavement and annihilation.* Most mystics and masters have written sparingly on the subject; in fact, if one were to survey the entire stock of religious literature, one probably would find hardly a volume dealing directly with it.

Yet it is precisely here that the most important stage of the jour-ney is completed. Attar has said that "the essence of this valley is forgetfulness, dumbness, deafness, and distraction."[1] The Sufi saint Chiragh-i-Delhi describes this phase as *continuity of affliction* leading to the dread of losing the Beloved's love, which leads to *obliteration,* and finally destruction. Although this exalted state is quite beyond the conception of the mind, and hence even descriptions of these states must be grossly inadequate, the saints and mystics have spo-ken metaphorically of these profound changes and transformations.

Here, as Attar has said, the world becomes but a play of shadows in the immensity of "a single ray of the celestial sun."[2]

This stage has also been likened to an immense ocean, which begins to heave, causing its surface patterns to lose their form. The form and pattern are none other than the present world and the world to come. When in this state, the lover is reduced to ashes and nothing of him or her remains.

A story describes how someone once saw Majnun making an image of Leila and himself in the soil. Then Majnun effaced the image of Leila. The passerby remarked, "What sort of love is it which makes the lover efface the sketch of the Beloved?"

Majnun said in reply, "If you do not find Leila in me, then make another sketch of her." A poet wrote of this story:

When someone carves the lover's image
The Beloved emerges out of it.[3]

Continuity of Affliction

Ahmad Ghazzali has given us profound insight into the psychology of the transformative search for the Beloved. In this final state, approaching union, the sign of "love's perfection is that the Beloved becomes the lover's affliction, so that he or she cannot possibly have the strength to bear her and cannot carry her weight, and he stands waiting by the door of annihilation."[4] In this state, the lover finds rest neither in the presence of the Beloved nor away from Her. In this paradox of existence, the knot of unity is finally tied. In the end, the "continuity of affliction" produces "the continuity of seeing." The poet speaks of this enigma when he says:

No one is like me so miserable,
For I am in grief both when I see you
And when I see you not.[5]

Love, then, in its near perfect state, is when the form of the Beloved becomes the image of the lover's spirit. When love reaches its perfect state, it subsists through and of itself, without anything outside it, including the Beloved. Until love is subsisting within itself, there is still not perfect love.

There are three unique phases to the binding of consciousness to itself. Here the lover has dissolved into the ocean of Light and love and the shores of self-existence can no longer be seen. The first phase, as has already been intimated, is when the lover reaches that state of purity of which Darshan Singh writes:

I have reached that state of bliss,
that state of ecstasy, that state of perfect peace,
that state of self-oblivion
where there is only Sawan [his Beloved]
there is no trace of me.[6]

In this state, the mind of the lover is so pure that it functions as the mirror of the Beloved. A Muslim divine describes this state as follows:

The place inside is so filled with my Beloved
That there is no room for me.
In you am I, look in my eyes and see the Oneness.
If you do not see, am I to be blamed?[7]

In the middle phase, mystical knowledge is added to the experience of union. Yet this knowledge is not of an objectifiable reality, but of a noetic, nondual oneness. Here, the lover who is now the Beloved contemplates himself or herself in the mirror of never-ending oneness. Here the lover is given knowledge that he or she is in a state of union. Although from an ordinary point of view, it would appear that such a state would imply the positionality of subject and object; in fact, subject and object are identified with one another.

This phase has been described by the poets as "drinking wine and being told they are becoming drunk." In this state, the lover experiences himself or herself as the Beloved, but also sees his or her own form within the Beloved's. Speaking of this rare experience, Kabir said:

> *One entered all,*
> *All entered that.*
> *Kabir entered knowledge.*
> *No duality.*[8]

Obliteration

The last phase of the state of union is in fact the only real union, for here the ultimate ontological reality is reached, which is the obliteration of both subject and object. In this state, there is no sign of either the Beloved or the lover, for both, as explained earlier, are branches of the tree of love itself. At this stage, there is only undifferentiated awareness, not of anything, but in an absolute sense of itself being nothing else but love.

The concept of annihilation or obliteration is a difficult one for Western readers. Such negative imagery often brings to mind thoughts of total extinction or lifelessness. Terms like "annihilation" may, to our ears, set up a sense of dualism that does not reflect the essential oneness of love.

For the lover, the experience of divine love is always one of expansiveness and inclusivity, even in its initial stages. True love can never be confined within any boundaries and defies the dualism of "I" and "other." Annihilation in this phase indicates the obliteration of a sense of separate existence, conditioned by the illusory experience of mind and matter. The cosmic embrace with divine love obliterates every aspect of limitation and reveals the Self as the primordial reality. Sant Darshan gives us a wonderful depiction of this state:

What does it matter if I am called a man?
In reality I am the very soul of love.
The entire earth is my home,
and the universe my country.[9]

Mystic poets Rumi, Sant Darshan Singh, Farid Attar, Hildegard of Bingen, Meister Eckhart, Kabir, and many others have testified to the wonderful, incomprehensible essence of this Being whose presence consumes a hundred thousand worlds in a moment. Despite the outer shell of differences in language, culture, and religion, the experience of unity defies cultural and religious singularities. Meister Eckhart says:

In this breaking-through I find that God and I
are both the same.
Then I am what I was, I neither wax nor wane,
for I am the motionless cause that is moving all things.[10]

The obliteration of differentiation is, in essence, the nature of realization. The Yoga Darshana describes it thus: "When alone the object of contemplation remains and one's form is annihilated, this is known as identification."[11] The Buddha insisted upon a nondual reality as the primary characteristic of realization. The Buddhist does not speak of "love" but of "emptiness." This no-thingness is itself pure awareness. Of what, one may ask? It is awareness of itself. Sengtsan says, "In the World of Reality there is no self, there is no other than Self." All beings are "the Buddha nature."[12]

Union

Sant Rajinder Singh reminds us of the nature of ultimate mystical union when he says, "The mystical journey takes us where opposites reveal themselves as one."[13] The entire journey is a journey in Love by love and back to Love. Since God is love, love must love. And to "love," there must be a Beloved. But as God is eternal infinite existence, there is no one for Him to love but Himself. And to love himself, he must imagine himself as the Beloved whom he as the lover imagines he loves.

But the "beloved" and "lover" imply separation. This separation implies longing; and longing causes search for what one is missing. The greater and more intense the lover's search, the greater and more terrible the longing the lover must undergo.

When longing reaches its uttermost limits, separation's purpose is complete. The purpose of separation was that Love might experience itself as lover and Beloved and come to know itself as Love.

When Union is attained, the lover now knows he was all along the Beloved, lover and love all in one. In fact, every stage of the journey was a journey of lover trying to overcome the illusion of separation from itself.

In the final analysis, there is no analysis possible. Love is beyond all questions and all answers; *love is that which is, and it is.* Since these states are not rational, the mystic writers merely point to reassuring signs along the road for those who have entered upon the Great Journey. Lao Tzu recognized this paradoxical dilemma when he says in the Tao Te Ching (LXXI):

Not knowing that one knows is best
Thinking that one knows when one does not know is sickness.[14]

Kabir, finding it impossible to describe, said:

If I say it's one, it isn't so.
If I say it's two, it's slander.
Kabir has thought about it.
As it is,
So it is.[15]

It is this truth that all realization is meant to attain. The final attainment, in fact, is no attainment at all; it is merely the removal of illusion. The Supreme Godhead, the essence of Love, is a state beyond conceptualization. Sant Kirpal Singh explains that even the full effulgence of light, referred to as *sach khand* in the Sikh scriptures, *maqam i Haq* by the Sufi masters, and *Theosis* by Esoteric Christians, is not the final realization. As he notes, "in the higher planes of *Sat naam* [literally, "place of truth"], the soul goes on being absorbed until it comes into the wordless state, where there is no light or sound."

Of this placeless place or stateless state, very little can be said. In the prologue to the Sikh scriptures, Guru Nanak, the first guru of the Sikhs, gives us a poetic summary of the infinite existence of the Supreme Being who is love:

> *There is One Reality, the Unmanifest-manifest.*
> *Ever-Existent, He is Naam* [conscious spirit].
> *The creator pervading all;*
> *Without fear, without enmity;*
> *The Timeless; the Unborn; and the Self-existent;*
> *Complete within itself.*[16]

Other masters, mystics, and saints have, in their own ways, sought to explain this "Mysterium Magnum." Meister Eckhart used much the same words to describe the same realization:

> *What is the last end?*
> *It is the mystery of the darkness of the eternal Godhead*
> *which is unknown and never has been known.*
> *Therein, God abides to Himself unknown.*[17]

Using Sufi terminology, the Sufi Master Jili replies:

> *The Divine Obscurity is the primordial place,*
> *Where the suns of beauty set.*
> *It is the Self of God Himself.*[18]

Or again, should we have any doubt, these mystics' words are reinforced by another great Christian mystic, Jacob Boehme: "God has made all things out of nothing, and that same nothing is Himself."

Plato, too, glimpsed this reality: "There abides the very being with which true knowledge is concerned: the colorless, formless, intangible essence...knowledge absolute is existence absolute."[19]

And finally in the *Sefer Yetsirah*, with classical rabbinical humor and simplicity, it is written: "Before the One, what is there to count."[20]

What, then, is the consummation of the lover-Beloved relationship? Who is the lover? The lover is pure essence. What is love? It is the subsistence of the essence of things. The Sufi saint Jami explains the ontological beginning of this relationship in one of his poems:

Non-existence fell in love with Existence.
The Non-existent through this Love became existent.
Then non-existence was graced with
the Light of Existence,
its aspiration moved to its source.
The attraction of love holds together
the shadow and the sun.[21]

Who then is the lover but the Beloved in disguise? What then is the Beloved but the essence of love? What, we might ask, could arise out of truth, save truth? Indeed, what can possibly rise out of love, save love?

Love is the hidden secret about which it is said in the Qur'an, "I was a hidden treasure and desired to be loved. Therefore I created man." Jami and many others see love as the primal attribute of the Divine Essence. In truth, God is making love unto Himself, by Himself, and to Himself endlessly. When in pretemporality, before the appearance of creation, love was both essence and attribute, and yet causeless and without beginning.

For God to know and experience His own essence, as some Sufis have said, otherness was required. This otherness was itself latent in the very nature of love. It was not need, because perfect love is without need, complete in itself. In its expression as otherness, as lover and Beloved, what was latent in love became manifest. One lover, whose name is unknown, has tried to capture this paradox:

> *The almighty loved Himself, if ye should know*
> *Made the universe His own mirror to see Himself aright,*
> *Displayed His beauty to Himself.*
> *Really He is the lover, the Beloved and Love itself.*[22]

And Rumi tells us again:

> *The Beloved is all in all, the Lover only veils Him,*
> *The Beloved is all that lives, the lover only a dead thing.*[23]

God beholds His own beauty and loves it, and this we may call love in post-temporality. Love, then, in quite a paradoxical way, is not characterized by either union or separation. The experience of union is the attribute of the Beloved, while the experience of separation is the attribute of the lover. Love is freed from the domains of union or separation and is beyond time and cause but is itself the cause of all.

Primordial Beginning

We have arrived, then, at the primordial beginning, because in love the end must become the beginning, for there is neither beginning nor end. As Sant Darshan has remarked, "Love has only a beginning, it has no end."[24] The journey through time from pre-temporality to post-temporality is a journey through the illusion of duality. It is a movement through "existence" to "beingness," from form to formlessness. The journey of love is implied not only in every creature, but also in every atom of creation, for the source of otherness, whether an atom or a sun, lies in pretemporality and henceforth. Rumi expressed this wonderfully:

When was I ever less by dying...
Yet once more I shall die as man, to soar,
With angels blessed; but even from angelhood
I must pass on; all except God doth perish.
When I have sacrificed my angel-soul,
I shall become what no mind ever conceived.
Oh let me not exist; for nonexistence
Proclaims in organ tones, "To Him we shall return."[25]

After arriving at their final destination, the lover, according to the Sufi saint Ibn Arabi, is "then made to remain, then gathered together...then assigned." One who "remains" at the destination is called "one who stops."[26] These great souls do not return with a mission from God but remain absorbed in God.

Those who are "assigned" return to the world of creation to do the work of perfecting souls and bringing them back to their Source. Sant Kirpal Singh has distinguished two types of beings who "return." First are the *Swateh Sant Gurus*, who come into the world as perfected beings and need no further training. They are the spiritual guides of all humanity, carefully tending to the spiritual evolution of all sentient beings. The second are *Sants*, who complete the course of perfection during their current lifetime. The only difference is that one comes with authority, while the other "acquires authority while here."[27] Both, however, come with a mission and work selflessly and tirelessly for the salvation of humankind by the authority of the Supreme Being.

Such perfected beings remain perpetually thirsty. For the journey *to* God is limited, as it means crossing the ocean of existence. But the journey *in* God is infinite, because His attributes are endless and without limit.[28] So satiation is unimaginable to the perfect beings of God. And this final journey we speak of is in God, through God, and by God.

Chapter Twelve
Death:
The Final Beginning

But when this perishable will have put on the imperishable,
and this mortal will have put on immortality,
then will come about the saying that is written,
"Death is swallowed up in victory."
"O death, where is your victory? O death, where is your sting?"
—I Cor. 15:54–55

The above words sum up the life of the true lover and mystic not only during this life, but at the moment of final departure from this world as well.

At every moment, the mystic lover is crying out, "O death, I am to thee a death," for in dying to his or her small self, the true Self may be born. But the paradox of the lover's path is precisely this: At every moment of death, there is a corresponding moment of birth, and the two are quite interdependent. It is only in the final death, that the soul, as the Sufis say, "passes away into God," where there is no further transformation. At that moment, there is only God, the self-existent, eternal, and immutable mystery of pure Being.

For the lover, all births and all deaths are part of a progression toward pure Being. Though powerful experiences on the human level, they are merely signposts, part of the changing panorama of illusion. Human death is simply a cousin to the inevitable final death in God, for to Him we must all finally return. The Qur'an (28:88) sums up the lover's understanding with these words: "All things perish save His countenance."

In this context, the process of initiation is seen as the first of many spiritual births of the lover, each one implying the death of an aspect of his or her illusory self. This first initiation is one in which the state of ignorance is first challenged by the force of love, for now the lover sees within himself the Light of God and knows he is of God and from God. In every subsequent initiation, love continues to challenge the forces of separation and duality; it beckons us on to ever more permanent states of being. While the lover remains living in this world, the true lover's life is infused with the unitive creative action of love on all levels. To live is to live in the Christ-like love of God, as Saint Paul has wonderfully said: "For to me, to live is Christ and to die is gain" (Phil. 1:21 ESV).

Dying Daily

Death, for the mystic, is a way of life, in which all things are consumed in the great fire of love. The real lover is one who already has died to his or her physical body, and traverses freely into other worlds unfettered by earthly encumbrances. He or she further dies to his or her astral body and finally to his or her causal body, each of which represents a further transition from illusion to reality, from death to immortality, and from separation to unity. Throughout mystic literature and poetry, the lover is portrayed as one who has already died. Prophet Mohammed exhorted his followers to "Die before you Die." By this he meant die to the "small self" (*nafs*, in Sufism) before you actually die physically. The death of the physical body is only a steppingstone to the fuller, freer, and richer life of the spirit. Rumi encapsulated this truth with the words:

> *One Reason to gain eternal life*
> *tread everlastingly the way of death.*[1]

The practice of spiritual dying is as old as existence itself. Entering the spiritual path is a dying to our small selves. Every moment of our lives is asking that we die and die again to the illusion of separation. For in each death, the ego, which for the lover is the symbol of separation, is put to another death. Death, as Philalethes, the seventeenth-century English Hermetic philosopher, said, "must precede perfect union."[2]

It could be said that virtually every page of Meister Eckhart's works proclaims the death of the limited false personality. Ramana Maharshi has said, as have all the nondualists, that "one cannot see God and yet retain individuality."[3] The lover is one who has become an expert at annihilation, for it is only in annihilation "that we discover the beautiful face of the bride."[4]

The lane of love is very narrow; it admits only one. Annihilation then is the ending of the vast complex net of chains binding us to this temporal impermanent world of suffering. The divine lover, as we have seen in the preceding chapters, learns this art of dying while living so that there is absolutely nothing, not even his or her very self, to which he or she has not died. Death is both sign and symbol of the destruction of "I" consciousness. Sri Sankaracharya once said, "He is the knower of the Self to whom the ideas of 'me' and 'mine' have become quite meaningless."[5]

The Death of Saints

Those who have "broken this idol of clay," as Rumi put it, find the face of the Beloved gloriously before them. For the saints, the moment the soul leaves the body in physical death, it is reunited with the Divine Beloved. Death is the vehicle for the lover's final deliverance and union. Sant Kirpal Singh states the position of saints who have already "passed away in God":

The lovers know where and how to die,
They accept and relish death as a gift from the Beloved.

With inner eye opened, they see the glory of God,
When others are forced blindfolded
into the blind alley.[6]

Angelus Silesius wrote:

I say since death alone delivers me,
It is of all things the best of things.[7]

The Death of Distinction

The final death is the death of the distinction between life and death. Having eradicated within himself or herself the distinction between life and death, what is left for the lover is always a continuous beginning. For the love that dwells in unity, death is not opposed to love, but the mirror in which it is reflected. The lover who faces his or her end faces no end at all. He or she faces only the supreme Friend, and a new beginning.

Endnotes

Introduction

1. Darshan Singh, 1989, p. 22.
2. Meher Baba, 1966, p. 85.
3. Johnson, pp. 146–150.
4. De Rougemont, pp. 51–52.
5. Johnson, pp. 148–156.
6. Darshan Singh, 1989, p. 107.
7. Ibid., p. 95.
8. Darshan Singh, 1986, p. 2.
9. Valiuddin, p. 128.
10. Jeffares, p. 217.
11. Perry, p. 680.
12. Ibid., p. 634.
13. All biblical references are to the King James Version and the English Standard Edition and are cited hereafter in the text.
14. Nicholson, 1925–1940, vol. 2, verse 2328.
15. John Smith, 1821, p. 300.
16. Darshan Singh, 1978, p. 98.
17. Perry, p. 814.
18. Margaret Smith, 1950, p. 91.

Chapter 1

1. Darshan Singh, 1989, back cover.
2. Guénon, 1964, p. 273.
3. Evans, vol. I, p. 275.
4. Guénon, 1964, p. 219.
5. Rajinder Singh, p. 38.
6. Schaya, p. 73.

7. Kirpal Singh, *Sat Sandesh*, August 1971, p. 2.
8. Hayat, p. 1.
9. Goswami, p. 79.
10. Weninger.
11. Whinfield & Kazvine, p. idem XII.
12. Perry, p. 628.
13. Evans, vol. I, p. 294.
14. Browne, vol. II, p. 268.
15. Darshan Singh, 1986, p. 4.
16. Darshan Singh, 1978, p. 249.
17. Dermenghem, n.d., p. 348.
18. Valiuddin, p. 32.
19. Darshan Singh, 1986, p. 24.
20. Valiuddin, p. 39.
21. Nicholson, 1925–1940, p. 1435.

Chapter 2
1. Perry, p. 23.
2. Kirpal Singh, 1967a, p. 59.
3. Ramdas, p. 255.
4. Dermenghem, n.d., p. 202.
5. Kirpal Singh, 1973, *Night*, p. 251.
6. Nicholson, 1925–1940, p. 2548.
7. Kirpal Singh, *Sat Sandesh*, November 1975, p. 4.
8. Begg, p. 148.
9. Sivananda, pp. 107–109.
10. Norton, p. 14.
11. Davis & Tsung, p. 111.
12. Sawan Singh, p. 54.
13. Venkataraman, pp. 499–500.
14. Pourjavady, p. 23.
15. Kirpal Singh, *Sat Sandesh*, November 1973, p. 2.
16. Valiuddin, p. 203.
17. Liguori, pp. 42–43.

Chapter 3
1. Valiuddin, p. 12.
2. Nott, p. 102.
3. Kirpal Singh, 1973, *Night*, p. 202.
4. Kirpal Singh, *Sat Sandesh*, June 1976, p. 30.
5. Ibid., pp. 30–31.
6. Valiuddin, p. 15.
7. Clissold, pp. 40–41.
8. Perry, p. 493.
9. Yutang, p. 235.
10. Nicholson, 1911, p. 299.
11. Darshan Singh, 1986, p. 7.
12. Allchin, p. 161.

13. Schuon, p. 145.
14. Gibran, part 5, chapter 41.

Chapter 4
1. Darshan Singh, 1986, p. 27.
2. Valiuddin, p. 168.
3. Valiuddin, p. 24.
4. Pourjavady, p. 44.
5. Underhill, p. 131.
6. Shastri, p. 132.
7. Kirpal Singh, *Sat Sandesh*, January 1971, p. 12.
8. Ibid., p. 12.
9. Hess & Singh, p. 82.
10. Darshan Singh, 1978, pp. 252–253.
11. Valiuddin, p. 13.
12. Margaret Smith, 1959, pp. 275–278.

Chapter 5
1. Darshan Singh, 1986, p. 34.
2. Nott, p. 102
3. Epstein, pp. 126–127.
4. Kirpal Singh, *Sat Sandesh*, April 1974, p. 5.
5. Pourjavady, p. 18.
6. Hess & Singh, p. 34.
7. Kirpal Singh, 1973, *Night*, p. 258.
8. Wilber, p. 63.
9. Valiuddin, p. 38.
10. Pourjavady & Wilson, p. 81.
11. Pourjavady, p. 46.
12. Bahari, p. 61.
13. Coomaraswamy, 1948, pp. 20–21.
14. Meher Baba, 1967, p. 9.

Chapter 6
1. Darshan Singh, 1986, p. 39.
2. De Courteille, p. 172.
3. Baba Sawan Singh, the esteemed 20th-century saint known as the Master of Surat Yoga.
4. Rodriguez & Kavanaugh, Book 2, chapter 5, chapter 9.
5. Darbandi & Davis, p. 180.
6. Pourjavady, p. 66.
7. Darshan Singh, 1978, p. 248.
8. Ibid., p. 249.
9. Ibid., p. 249.
10. Ibid., p. 250.
11. Valiuddin, p. 21.

Chapter 7
1. Darshan Singh, 1989, p. 7.
2. Kirpal Singh, *Sat Sandesh*, October 1976, pp. 10–11.
3. Pourjavady, p. 23.
4. Ibid., p. 24.
5. Kempis, vol. 7, p. III.
6. Venkataraman, p. 303.
7. Lederer, p. 77.
8. Herbert, p. 28.
9. Nicholson, 1952, Divan Tabriz XXXXI.
10. Themi, p. 158.
11. Nott, p. 110.

Chapter 8
1. Darshan Singh, 1989, p. 30
2. Nott, p. 116.
3. Valiuddin, p. 20.
4. Stein, p. 16.
5. Hume, pp. vi, xi, 3.
6. Goddard, p. vii.
7. Muller, pp. 153–154.
8. Houston, p. 134.
9. Frank, p. 49.
10. Nott, p. 117.
11. Nikhilanada, p. 223.
12. Pourjavady & Wilson, p. 85.

Chapter 9
1. Darshan Singh, 1986, p. 21.
2. Hess & Singh, p. 58.
3. Nakosteen, p. 341.
4. Hess & Singh, p. 103.
5. Menzies, p. 22.
6. Valiuddin, p. 12.
7. Ibid., p. 13.
8. Kadloubovsky & Palmer, p. 258.
9. Margaret Smith, 1950, p. 72.
10. Kirchberger, p. 63.
11. Evans, vol. I, p. 37.
12. Fitzgerald, verse 59.
13. Dermenghem, 1931, p. 110.
14. Coomaraswamy, 1947, p. 100.
15. Darshan Singh, 1977, p. 49.
16. Nikhilananda, p. 346.
17. Pourjavady & Wilson, p. 44.
18. Kristello, p. 228.
19. Darshan Singh, 1986, p. 25.

20. Pourjavady & Wilson, pp. 44–45.
21. Nicholson, 1952, verse xxxii.

Chapter 10
1. Darshan Singh, 1989, p. 51.
2. Nott, p. 119.
3. Pourjavady & Wilson, p. 86.
4. Valiuddin, p. 29.
5. Pourjavady & Wilson, p. 87.
6. Hess & Singh, p. 106.
7. Meher Baba, 1967, *Discourses*, p. 163.
8. Kirpal Singh, 1973, *Night*, p. 272.
9. Nott, p. 123.
10. Kirpal Singh, 1967a, p. 119.
11. Meher Baba, 1963, p. 17.
12. Scholem, p. 39, p. 223.
13. Rajinder Singh, p. 49.
14. Pourjavady & Wilson, p. 39.

Chapter 11
1. Nott, p. 123.
2. Ibid., p. 126.
3. Pourjavady & Wilson, p. 68.
4. Ibid., p. 69.
5. Ibid., p. 69.
6. Darshan Singh, 1986, p. 55.
7. Kirpal Singh, 1973, *Night*, p. 277.
8. Hess & Singh, pp. 121–122.
9. Darshan Singh, 1986, p. 55.
10. Evans, p. 221.
11. Danielou, p. 221.
12. Franck, p. 5.
13. Rajinder Singh.
14. Ta-Kao, Tao Te Ching, LXXI
15. Hess & Singh, p. 103.
16. Kirpal Singh, 1981, p. 87.
17. Evans, p. 224.
18. Burckhardt, p. 54.
19. Jowett, p. 247.
20. Guénon, 1931, p. 45.
21. Whinfield & Kazvine, p. xii.
22. Valiuddin, p. 129.
23. Valiuddin, p.130.
24. Darshan Singh, 1986, p. 2.
25. Kirpal Singh, 1967b, p. 26.
26. Harris, p. 48.
27. Kirpal Singh, 1967a, pp. 17–18.
28. Harris, p. 64.

Chapter 12

1. Nicholson, 1925, p. 206.
2. Hermetic Museum, vol. II, p. 255.
3. Venkataraman, p. 571.
4. Nicholson, 1952, verse XLII.
5. Jagadanada, pp. xvi, 29.
6. Kirpal Singh, 1973, *Night*, p. 92.
7. Silesius, vol. IV, p. 101.

References

Sacred Texts

All biblical references are to the King James Version and the English Standard Edition.

Holy Qur'ān (M. H. Shakir, Trans.). Elmhurst, NY: Tahrike Tarsile Qur'ān, 1999.

The Holy Qur'ān (Abdullah Yusuf Ali, Trans.). Brentwoord, MD: Amana, 1987.

The Holy Qur'ān (Maulana Muḥammad Ali, Trans.). Lahore, India: Ahmadiyyah Anjuman Isha'at Islam, 1995.

Books and Articles

Allchin, F. R. (Trans.). (1964). Tulsi Das, *Kavitavali.* London, UK: G. Allen and Unwin.

Bahari, B. (1971). *Mystic, saints, and masters.* Delhi, India: Bharitiya Vidya Bhavan.

Begg, W. D. (1977). *Hazrat khawaj moinindin chisti.* Tucson, AZ: Chisti Sufi Mission of America.

Browne, E. G. (1902). *Literary history of Persia.* London, UK: T. F. Unwin.

Burckhardt, T. (Trans.). (1953). *De l'homme universal [al-insan al-Kamil,* Arabic]. Lyon, France: P. Derain.

Chanan, M. D. (Trans.). (1983). *Ha zohar book of splendor.* New York, NY: Paulist Press.

Clissold, S. (1977). *The wisdom of the Spanish mystics.* New York, NY: New Directions.

Coomaraswamy, Ananda. (1947). *Am I my brother's keeper?* New York, NY: John Day.

Coomaraswamy, Ananda. (1948). *Hinduism and buddhism.* New York, NY: Philosophical Library.

Danielou, A. (1949). *Yoga: The method of re-integration.* London, UK: Christopher Johnson Press.

Darbandi, A. & Davis, D. (Trans.). (1984). Farid ud-Din Attar, *The conference of the birds*. New York, NY: Penguin.

Davis, T. L., & Tsung, C. Y. (Trans.). (1939). Chang Po-Tuan, Essay on the understanding of truth. *Proceedings of the American Academy of Science, 73*(5).

De Courteille, P. (Trans.). (1917). Farid ud-din Attar, *Memorial of the saints*. London: Royal Asiatic Society.

Dermenghem, E. (n.d.). *Vies de saints musalmans*. Algiers: Editions Bacconier.

Dermenghem, E. (1931). *L'eloge du vin*. Paris, France: Editions Vega.

De Rougemont, D. (1956). *Love in the western world* (M. Belgion, Trans.). New York, NY: Pantheon.

Epstein, P. (2001). *Kabbalah: The way of the Jewish mystic*. New York, NY: Shambhala.

Evans, C. de B. (Trans.). (1924). *Meister Eckhart, by Franz Pfeiffer,* Leipzig, 1857. London, UK: J. M. Watkins.

Fitzgerald, E. (Trans.) (1859). Omar Khayyam, *Rubaiyat*. London, UK: Bernard Quaritch.

Franck, F. (1976). *The book of angelus silesius*. New York, NY: Knopf.

Gibran, K. (1928). *Jesus the son of man, His words and His deeds as told and recorded by those who knew Him*. New York, NY: Knopf.

Goddard, D. (Ed.). (1938). *Lankavatara sutra: A Buddhist bible*. Thetford, VT: Dwight Goddard.

Goswami, Shrivatsa. (1987). *The divine consort* (J. S. Hawley & D. M. Wolf, Eds.). Boston, MA: Beacon Press.

Guénon, R. (1931). *Le symbolisme de la croix*. Paris, France: Editions Vega.

Guénon, R. (1964). *Aperçus l'initiation*. Paris, France: Editions Traditionelles.

Harris, T. (Trans.). (1981). Ibn Arabi, *Journey to the lord of power*. New York, NY: Inner Traditions.

Hayat, Mir Muhammad. (1906). *Misbah-ul-hayut*. Bombay, India: Fat-hul-furim Press.

Herbert, J. (Trans.). (1943). Ananda Moyi, *Aux sources de la joie*. Calcutta, India: Ophyris.

Hermetic Museum. (1953). *A short vade mecum to the celestial ruby*. London, UK: Vincent Stuart and John Watkins.

Hess, L., & Singh, S. (Trans). (1983). *The bijak of Kabir*. San Francisco, CA: North Point Press.

Hobhouse, S. (Ed.). (1938). *The selected mystical writings of William Law*. London, UK: C. W. Daniel.

Houston, J. (1987). *The search for the beloved*. New York, NY: Tarcher Press.

Hume, R. E. (Trans.). (1934). *The thirteen principal Upanishads*. New York, NY: Oxford University Press.

Ibn al-Farid. (1931). Khamriyya, *L'eloge du vin*. Paris, France: Editions Vega.

Jagadanada, Swami (Trans.). (1949). Sri Sankaracharya, *Upadeshasahasri, a thousand teachings*. Madras, India: Sri Ramakrishna Math.

Jeffares, A. N. (1968). *A commentary on the collected poems of W.B. Yeats*. Stanford, CA: Stanford University Press.

Johnson, R. (1983). *We: Understanding the psychology of romantic love*. New York, NY: Harper Row.

Jowett, B. (Trans.). (1953). *"Phaedrus" dialogues of Plato* (4th ed.). Oxford, UK: Clarendon Press.

Kadloubovsky, E., & Palmer, G. E. H. (Trans). (1951). *Saint Isaac of Syria, writings from the philokalia on the prayer of the heart.* London, UK: Faber and Faber.

Kempis, Thomas à. (n.d). *The imitation of Christ.* New York, NY: Thomas Y. Crowell

Kirchberger, C. (Trans.). (1957). *Richard of Saint Victor.* London, UK: Faber and Faber.

Kristello, P. O. (1943). *Philosophy of Marsilio Ficino.* New York, NY: Columbia University Press.

Lederer, F. (Trans.). (n.d.). Shabistari, *The secret rose garden, of Sai'd ud din Mahmud Shabistari.* Lahore, India: Ashraf Publications.

Liguori, A. (1935). *Conformity to the will of god.* Clyde, MO: Benedictine Convent of Perpetual Adoration.

Meher Baba. (1963). *The everything and the nothing.* Sydney, Australia: Meher House Press.

Meher Baba. (1966). *Meher Baba on love.* Poona, India: Baba Publishing.

Meher Baba. (1967). *Discourses of Baba.* Tokyo, Japan: Komiyama Press.

Menzies, L. (Trans.). (1953). Mechthild of Magdeburg, *The revelations of Mechthild of Magdeburg.* London, UK: Longmans Green.

Muller, M. (Trans.). (1898). *The Dhammapada (Sacred books of the east,* Vol. 10). Oxford, UK: Clarendon Press.

Nakosteen, M. (Trans.). (1973). *Divan of Hafiz.* Boulder, CO: University of Colorado Press.

Nicholson, R. A. (Trans). (1911). Ali Hujiwir, *Khasf al mahjub.* London: Luzac Press.

Nicholson, R. A. (Trans). (1925–1940). *Mathnawi of Jalalu'ddin Rumi* (Gibb Memorial Series). London, UK: Luzac.

Nicholson, R. A. (Trans.). (1952). *Selected poems from the Divani Shamsi Tabriz.* Cambridge, MA: University Press.

Nikhilanada, Swami. (Trans.) (1942). *The gospel of Sri Ramakrishna.* New York, NY: RamaKrishna Vedanta Center.

Norton, T. (1928). *Ordinall of alchemy.* London, UK: Edward Arnold.

Nott, C. S. (Trans.) (1969 [1954]). Farid-uddin Attar, *Conference of the birds.* New York, NY: Samuel Weiser.

Perry, W. N. (1971). *A treasury of traditional wisdom.* New York, NY: Simon Schuster.

Pourjavady, N. (Trans). (1986). Ahmad Ghazzali, *Sawanih, Bayazid al Bistami.* London, UK: Routledge and Paul Kegan/Iran University Press.

Pourjavady, N., & Wilson, P. (Trans.). (1987). *The drunken universe: An anthology of Persian Sufi poetry.* Grand Rapids, MI: Phanes Press.

Ramdas, Swami. (1955). *World is God.* Kanhangad, India: Ananda Ashram.

Rodriguez , O., & Kavanaugh, K. (Trans). (1991). *Collected works of Saint John of the Cross.* Washington, DC: ICS Publications.

Schaya, L. (1958). *L'homme et l'absolu selon la kabbale.* Paris, France: Buchet/Chastel.

Scholem, G. (1954). *Major trends in Jewish mysticism.* New York, NY: Schocken Books.

Schuon, F. (1961). *Stations of wisdom.* London, UK: John Murray.

Shastri, H. P. (Trans.). (1952). Yoga Vasishtha, *The world within the mind.* London, UK: Shanti Sadan Press.

Silesius, Angelus. (n.d.). *Cherubinischer Wandersmann.* Paris, France: Aubier Editions Montaigne.

Singh, Darshan. (1977). *The cry of the soul.* Bowling Green VA: SK Publications.
Singh, Darshan. (1978). *Secret of secrets.* Bowling Green, VA: SK Publications.
Singh, Darshan. (1986). *A tear and a star.* Delhi, India: Sawan Kirpal Publications.
Singh, Darshan. (1989). *Love at every step.* Delhi, India: Sawan Kirpal Publications.
Singh, Kirpal. (1961). *The crown of life.* Bowling Green, VA: SK Publications.
Singh, Kirpal. (1967a). *Godman.* Delhi, India: Ruhani Satsang.
Singh, Kirpal. (1967b). *The mystery of death.* Delhi, India: Ruhani Satsang.
Singh, Kirpal. (1971, January). *Sat sandesh* [periodical]. Tilton, NH: Sant Bani Press.
Singh, Kirpal. (1973). *The night is a jungle.* Tilton, NH: Sant Bani Press.
Singh, Kirpal. (1973, November 10). *Sat Sandesh.* Tilton, NH: Sant Bani Press.
Singh, Kirpal. (1974, April). *Sat Sandesh.* Tilton, NH: Sant Bani Press.
Singh, Kirpal. (1975, November). *Sat Sandesh. Bowling Green VA: SK Publications.*
Singh, Kirpal. (1976, June). *Sat Sandesh.* Bowling Green, VA: Kirpal Publications.
Singh, Kirpal. (1976, October). *Sat Sandesh.* Tilton NH: Sant Bani Press.
Singh, Kirpal. (1981). *The Jap ji.* Bowling Green, VA: Kirpal Publications.
Singh, Rajinder. (2005). *Echoes of the divine.* Naperville IL: SK Publications.
Singh, Sawan. (1986). *A pictorial biography: Glimpses of the great master.* Hong Kong: Radha Swami Satsang Beas.
Sivananda. Swami. (1952). *Japa yoga.* Rishiskesh, India: Yoga Vedanta Forest University.
Smith, John. (1821). *Select discourses.* London, UK: Cambridge University Press.
Smith, Margaret. (1950). *Readings from the mystics of Islam.* London, UK: Luzac.
Smith, Margaret. (Trans.) (1959). Al Ghazzali, *Ihyu Ulum al-Din or the revivification of religion.* London, UK: Luzac.
Stein, L. (1943, Fall). Hasidic music. *Chicago Jewish Forum, 1.*
Ta-Kao, C. (Trans.). (1937). *Lao Tzu.* London, UK: Buddhist Lodge.
Themi (Trans.). (1970). *Sri Aurobindo or the adventure of consciousness.* Pondicherry, India: All India Press.
Underhill, E. (Ed.). (1951). *Saint John of Ruysbroeck, The adornment of spiritual marriage* (C. A. Wynschenk, Trans.). London, UK: John M. Watkins.
Valiuddin, Mir. (1972). *Love of God.* Farnham, UK: Sufi Publishing.
Venkataraman, T. N. (Ed. & Trans.). (1955). *Talks with Sri Ramana Maharshi* (3 vols). South India: Tiruvannamalai.
Weninger, F. X. (1877). Catherine of Sienna, virgin. Retrieved from: http://catholicharboroffaithandmorals.com
Whinfield, E. H., & Kazvine, M. M. (Trans.). (1928). *Lawa'ih* [Flashes of divine light]. London, UK: Royal Asiatic Society Press.
Wilber, K. (1979). *No boundary.* Los Angeles, CA: Center Publishing House.
Yeats, W. B. (2007). *The tower (1928): Manuscript materials* (R. J. Finneran, Ed.). Ithaca, NY: Cornell University Press.
Yutang, L. (1951). *My country and my people.* London, UK: Heinemann Press.

About the Author

Andrew Vidich Ph.D. is con-
sultant, international speaker, and
author of more than five books.
His books include Love is a Secret
(1990), He has co-edited (multi-
ple editors) a collection of writings
of the twentieth century Spiritual
Saint, Sant Kirpal Singh Ji entitled,
*The Spiritual Path: An Anthology of the
Writings by Sant Kirpal Singh.* He was
contributing author to *The Heart of the
Healer,* and most recently, *Light Upon*

Light: 5 Master Paths to Awaken the Mindful Self. His forthcoming book
entitled, *Let There be Light; Experiencing Inner Light Across the World's
Sacred Traditions* will be released in the fall of 2014.

Dr. Vidich has been an adjunct assistant professor of religion
at Manhattan College and Iona College in New York. He has been
an Instructional Coach and award winning teacher in the NYC
Department of Education for over 18 years.

He is a founding member of The Interfaith Council of New York a not-for-profit interfaith organization as well as a member of the council of trustees of The Temple of Understanding, an international interfaith organization, which promotes global interfaith understanding and cooperation.

Dr. Vidich is a member of the board of directors and public relations coordinator for the Science of Spirituality Meditation Center, in Amityville New York. He has been studying meditation for 43 years under the guidance of three world renowned Meditation Masters including His Holiness Sant Kirpal Singh Ji, Sant Darshan Singh Ji, and His Holiness Sant Rajinder Singh Ji Maharaj.